Endorsements

People Raising meets a critical need in the evangelical missions community. Putting this book into the hands of missionary appointees will relieve them of great uncertainties and provide valuable practical insights into how to raise their financial support.

Jim Reapsome
Executive Director, Evangelical Missions Quarterly

Immensely practical! I highly commend *People Raising* as a must for anyone preparing to raise support. Local church mission committees and mission agencies will find the book an invaluable tool in a rapidly changing world context.

Jerry Butler
Willow Creek Association

Thoroughly biblical and intensely practical, Bill Dillon provides the needed encouragement and instruction to anyone faced with the challenge of raising support. Here is a volume that cultivates positive attitudes and outlines twelve specific action steps that will bring support response. Support raising is turned from dread to delight.

J. Ronald Blue
President, CAM International

Bill Dillon has given us a book that many will find helpful in the process of raising up a support team. His positive attitude about the process, rather than looking on it as some form of drudgery, is refreshing. May this volume dispel the gloom and communicate to many the ministry they can have in this challenging process.

Richard Winchell
General Director, TEAM

William Dillon's book *People Raising* is long overdue. This practical book is a source of "know-how" and encouragement. I enthusiastically commend this book to veterans as well as new recruits.

George Sweeting
Chancellor, Moody Bible Institute

I recommend this book... not for your casual reading but for study and application. Much of what we teach to our new staff is contained in this book. The principles along with God's calling will allow many to be successful in this step of faith.

Steve Rentz
Campus Crusade for Christ

This should be a book of required reading and possibly a textbook in every Bible college and seminary training missionaries in cross-cultural studies.

Paul Alford
President, Toccoa Falls College

People Raising

A Practical Guide to Raising Support

by

William P. Dillon

MOODY PRESS
CHICAGO

About the Author

William Paul Dillon is a third-generation missions leader. His family began ministering in Chicago's inner city in 1918. Bill is married and has three children.

Bill is the founder and executive director of Inner City Impact, which ministers in Chicago's inner city and brings hope to the children, youth, and families who live there.

His education includes the following: B.A. in Bible theology, Moody Bible Institute, Chicago, Illinois; B.S. in business administration, Elmhurst College, Elmhurst, Illinois; M.B.A, Murray State University, Murray, Kentucky.

In addition to administrative and teaching skills, Bill has authored two books on basic Bible doctrine for children. He is a frequent speaker on college campuses, in churches, and for Christian ministries.

He has served on the following boards: Moody Bible Institute Alumni Association; former chairman of the board of the Association of North American Missions; former board member for AWANA Clubs, International.

Experienced in raising funds in the missionary arena for more than twenty years, Bill guides missionaries on a day-to-day basis. He has conducted numerous support-raising seminars for other Christian ministries and associations. In our tight economy, Bill bases his ministry on operating debt free.

Bill writes from experience and continues to raise funds for the cause of Christ. He also serves as a management and fundraising consultant for Resource Management Consultants.

This book is dedicated to those four very special people whom God has brought into my life to make up that unit called a family.

To my wife, Sandy, who joined me in 1972 on a journey of faith as we began the ministry of Inner City Impact on a sidewalk. We knew what it meant to operate a ministry with literally no resources—no meeting place, no staff, and no financial support. But the vision was alive in both of our hearts. She has not selfishly demanded of my time through the years of preparing this book but many times has urged me to "go for it."

To my three kids, Brian, Christina, and Bradley. They too have been patient and encouraging as Dad has sought to change people's lives. They are also very special, and I love them very much.

Table of Contents

Acknowledgments

I would like to express thanks to some of the people who have been instrumental in making this book a reality.

Special thanks to the board of Inner City Impact: Syl Chody, Tony Eager, Howard Eklind, Joe Irizarry, John Lockner, Bob Murfin, Don Raickett, and Mary Wade. They shared the vision of seeing this book completed and the value of sharing these ideas with missionaries all over the world.

To Joe De Kock and Abel David who taught me the computer skills that enabled me to produce what I learned and wanted to communicate to those going through the support process.

I am grateful to Stan Sharman, who came to my aid on many occasions, for his computer expertise.

Numerous people assisted in the typing of the book, including Cindie Anderson, Barbara Gemar, Sharon Murphy, Mike Murphy, Valerie Ash, Joan Layton, and Lyn Matejczyk.

Others helped in editing. John Lockner saw a very rough copy, and Judy Meyers, a friend throughout the years, helped edit and literally made the manuscript more reader friendly.

To Jeff Whetstone who lent his support with the graphics.

To Troy Philipps, former director of development at Inner City Impact, who allowed me to train and teach him the principles of support raising.

Preface

High atop the headquarters of Inner City Impact, nestled in an area that the *Chicago Tribune* refers to as one of the most dangerous communities in the United States, I answer the ringing phone in my office.

The voice on the other end fires a series of questions at me. I realize that he wants to be involved in our cause of bringing hope through the gospel to the children of the inner city. His final question: "Must I raise my support?"

When I respond affirmatively, the questioning abruptly ends, and another potential candidate is blown off the scene. He has heard the horror stories of raising support and doesn't want to go through the hassle that other potential missionaries are forced to endure.

Several months later another phone call comes. This time a pastor relates that a member of his congregation was accepted for missionary service by a respected evangelical mission. The prospective missionary has been raising support for eighteen months, but unable to meet the goal, he has withdrawn from missions.

It is painful to see the dwindling missionary market when never before have the fields been so ripe for harvest. Without an expanding work force, we will be unable to deliver the goods.

Part of the problem is the lack of an effective strategy for support raising. Too many missionaries struggle too hard to raise support. Is there a better way? Can mission organizations do more to equip missionaries to raise their support? How many potential missionaries give up before ever leaving their hometown?

Even more disturbing is the number of potential missionaries who never consider missions because they hear horror stories about support raising. They need to hear positive stories of those who have succeeded in raising the needed funds, who have made it to the field and are now getting the job done.

For years I have studied the efforts of missions and missionaries to raise support. Some have effective strategies, but they are few and far between.

I asked more than one hundred mission organizations to send materials they use to prepare missionary candidates. I also asked them to direct me to other missions that seemed to have a good handle on fund raising.

In some cases, I got what I expected: very little. In other cases, I was pleasantly surprised. The information I gathered, along with lessons learned through my own experience, is compiled in this book.

My goal in writing is to help the prospective or veteran missionary and mission organization to raise the prayer and financial support necessary for survival with as little effort as possible, in as short a time as possible, while solidifying friendships at the same time.

As you read, you will discover a purposeful strategy here. But recognize that our dependence is not on systems and strategies, but on the Lord. I am reminded that Psalm 147:10 -11 says, "His pleasure is not in the strength of the horse, nor his delight in the legs of a man; the Lord delights in those who fear him, who put their hope in his unfailing love."

With our hope rightly placed in a holy and awesome God, we can't go wrong. It is my prayer that the material that follows will help both the mission and the missionary as they endeavor to fulfill the Great Commission.

How to Use This Book

Different people in the mission community will glean from this book and use it as a tool to sharpen both the new and veteran missionary as they are involved in the ministry of support raising. To assist in that process, I've identified you in the process if you are a:

New missionary
Missionary preparing to go on home leave
Veteran missionary
Mission executive
Director of development
Mission personnel director or candidate secretary
Field director
Mission professor looking for a textbook on support raising
College placement personnel who counsel summer and career missionaries
Member of church missions committee
Pastoral staff who guides missionaries in support raising
Concerned Christian praying for those on the front line of world evangelism

Throughout the book you will find training suggestions. The suggestions are divided into two categories: Self-Guided Training, allowing a missionary to go through the material on his own at his own pace, and Group-Guided Training.

The ideal way to study this material is in a group setting. Individuals of the group study the Self-Guided Training, and the group together follows the recommendations for the Group-Guided Training. Much will be gained from interaction with the trainer, as well as from others in the group. Thus, this book serves as a guide to building a missionary support training program.

I advise you to read this book completely before implementing the recommended steps. Once you understand the total strategy, you will be ready to start at the beginning to implement the specific steps.

Cultivating a Positive Attitude Toward Support Raising

Chapter 1

When Andy received word that he had been accepted as a missionary, many thoughts ran through his mind. His initial excitement soon was replaced by a preoccupation with the negative aspects of raising support. Then Andy began to challenge the system itself. Why raise support? Why me?

Maybe you are considering missionary service, or maybe you have already been involved in the missionary enterprise for some time. In either case, the question, "Why raise support?" needs to be addressed.

I grew up in a missionary home where I saw faith at work. I attended the Moody Bible Institute and heard every conceivable missionary message. I talked with many missionaries and read missionary biographies. However, it was not until I personally raised support for our ministry that I comprehended the many important reasons for developing a base of consecrated supporters. In the past twenty years, I have come to understand that raising support is necessary for many reasons.

Support Raising Attracts a Base of Prayer Support

If you worked on our staff at Inner City Impact in a salaried position, few people would commit themselves to pray for you. However, when you serve in a missionary capacity, the people who invest financially in you are inclined to pray for you. Prayer follows financial investment.

Support Raising Stretches the Missionary's Faith

I like what David Tucker of Regions Beyond Missionary Union International says about deputation: "You are about to embark on what can be one of the most maturing and spiritually fulfilling ventures of your life."

Support raising can be a spiritual adventure. You'll love many aspects of it. But we do not grow and mature through that which is easy. When friends whom you expected to take on your support do not, it's discouraging. When days go by and your support level does not increase, you may be tempted to question your call to missionary service. Those are the days that you step forward in faith that God has called you and that in His time He

3

will supply every need. Raising support will teach you what it means to walk by faith.

Support Raising Stimulates and Encourages Missionary Vision in the Body of Christ

No doubt the best recruiter for missions is the missionary himself. Support raising calls for the missionary to interface with other believers who make up the body of Christ. When they meet face-to-face, the missionary communicates his vision, his call. His enthusiasm and dedication stimulate interest and involvement in missions.

In his article titled, "The Tin-Cup Image Can Be Shattered," Daniel Bacon looks at the missionary who raises support and sees him accomplishing three goals.

First, the missionary is a *model* for missions. That may seem scary, but you must never forget that God has given you your status as a missionary. In essence, you are a walking testimony of God's coveted plan for world evangelism. Bacon says, "The presence of a missionary is a living illustration of obedience to the Great Commission." In raising support, you keep God's priority of missions in front of the body of Christ, and you help them become mission-minded.

Second, the missionary becomes a *mobilizer* for missions. Financially and through prayer you provide believers the opportunity to participate in God's program for world evangelism. Because of your deputation ministry, some may sense God's heart for mission and join the missionary work force.

Third, the missionary serves as a *minister* for missions. You facilitate effective communication that will bring together the mission agency and the local church. Bacon says, "The missionary obviously needs the church for support, but the church needs the missionary to extend, in obedience to the Great Commission, its ministry worldwide."[1] We will talk more about opportunities to minister later in the book.

Support Raising Broadens the Base of Financial Support for the Mission

If the average mission board were to hire missionaries based on its financial resources, there would be only a handful of missionaries throughout the world. Rather, the mission counts on the missionary through his network of people to broaden its financial base. When your friends support you, you play an integral part in broadening your mission's financial base.

Support Raising Develops You as a Person

Bud Taylor, of Source of Light Ministries, International, comments on what you learn as you raise support: "There are many things that God will teach you in His School of Deputation that you could not possibly learn anywhere else. During deputation you learn how to work with people and how to adapt under divergent, difficult, and sometimes desperate circumstances. That is when the realization dawns that we are so limited and God is so limitless!

"Deputation is not as is so often misrepresented a punitive measure, but a privilege. It is not a promotional gimmick, but a prerequisite for a missionary career.

"In the process of deputation one learns poise, polish, and proficiency and how to use time, tact, and talent to [one's] best advantage."[2]

Support Raising Stimulates Fellowship Among Other Believers

As the missionary contacts his network of people and adds friends to that network, he becomes involved with caring, praying, and burdened people. Sweet times of fellowship result as the missionary interacts with believers through support raising.

Support Raising Opens Opportunities to Witness

Support raising opens new horizons and contacts. As the missionary travels from place to place, God gives him divine appointments with the unsaved world. And through those opportunities, the missionary practices missions at home.

Scott Steele and Tom Frieze of International Missions provide perspective on the reason for support raising. "Missions was and is God's idea, and it is a real privilege to speak to God's people about God's program and to enlist their petitions."[3]

Support raising is far more than raising money. It is ministry. It is relationships. It is watching God work His eternal program for the ages in a practical way.

Self Guided Training

1. One value of support raising is that it stretches the faith of the missionary candidate. How would you like to see the Lord stretch your personal faith?

2. "Deputation is not as is often misrepresented a punitive measure, but a privilege." How do you see it as a privilege?

3. As you proceed through the process of raising support, you keep God's priority for missions in front of the body of Christ; you help fellow Christians become mission-minded. Write your vision of how God can use you to attract others to missions.

4. Identify three attitudes in you that might hinder your support raising.

1. In showing me that I have favor.
2. You get to be the "connector" between God's people, God's plan & His provision
3. By public speaking & living w/ Integrity
4. - People don't like to part w/ their $
- I don't know how
- I might do something wrong

Group
Guided

Training

1. Personally answer the questions above. Discuss them together in the group.

2. Invite a veteran missionary to talk about how support raising has been a ministry for him.

3. Invite a panel of missionaries to discuss ways to make support raising a ministry.

4. If the above two suggestions are not feasible, ask each group member to interview a missionary in person or by phone outside of class.

_____

_____

_____

_____

_____

_____

_____

Notes

1. Daniel W. Bacon, "The Tin-Cup Image Can Be Shattered," *Evangelical Missions Quarterly* 22, no. 4 (October 1986), 376.
2. Bud Taylor, *Taking the P.U. out of Deputation* (self-compiled pamphlet).
3. Scott Steele, *Scott Steele with Tom Frieze* (Reading: Pa.: International Missions).

Chapter 2

As Andy reflected on reasons raising support was necessary, he began to accept the fact that it was beneficial. But he still questioned whether it was biblical. He wondered if Scripture said anything about the process. Were there principles, commands, dos or don'ts, or any models in the Bible?

The Scriptures are not silent about finances.

Jesus spoke often concerning wealth, its use and its careless abuse. In fact, he spoke more directly about stewardship than about any other subject. Approximately seven hundred direct statements in the Bible relate to finances. One could add to this a hundred more indirect references, and nearly two-thirds of the parables Christ taught deal with the use of wealth. God often compares our use of wealth with our commitment to Him.[1]

God's Plan Calls for Others to Support Christian Workers

SIM indicates, "A review of Scripture reveals an amazing amount of material related to this subject. The following is an introduction to an interesting and valuable personal study."[2]

The Old Testament Pattern

In Numbers 18:21-24, we see the Old Testament pattern for support. God called for the nation of Israel to give a tithe to support their "full time" spiritual leaders. God never changed the plan, and the Old Testament ends with a stern rebuke to the nation for not giving these tithes (Mal. 3:8). This was God's plan, not something Moses or Aaron dreamed up.

I will give to the Levites all the tithes in Israel as their inheritance in return for the work they do while serving at the Tent of Meeting. From now on the Israelites must not go near the Tent of Meeting, or they will bear the consequences of their sin and will die. It is the Levites who are to do the work at the Tent of Meeting and bear the responsibility for offenses against it. This is a lasting ordinance for the generations to come. They will receive no inheritance among the Israelites. Instead, I give to the Levites as their inheritance the tithes that the Israelites present as an offering to the Lord. That is why I said concerning them: "They will have no inheritance among the Israelites." (Num. 18:21-24)

9

The New Testament Pattern

In Luke 8:1-3, we see the pattern for support illustrated in Jesus' life and ministry. He allowed others to minister to Him physically and materially. He was not embarrassed to receive help as they gave to Him of their substances (goods, possessions, and property).

"The Twelve were with Him" (Luke 8:1). The implication is that Jesus and the Twelve were giving themselves fully to ministering to people, and the people were providing for their needs.

> *After this, Jesus traveled about from one town and village to another, proclaiming the good news of the kingdom of God. The Twelve were with him, and also some women who had been cured of evil spirits and diseases: Mary (called Magdalene) from whom seven demons had come out; Johanna the wife of Cuza, the manager of Herod's household; Susanna; and many others. These women were helping to support them out of their own means. (Luke 8:1-3)*

The Twelve were sent out by direction from Jesus, not by their own choice or volition (Matt. 10:5). They were to give themselves fully to ministry, not to earning a living. They were not allowed to take food or money for operating expenses. Rather, they were to depend on God's supply, and God's plan for that provision was through other people (vv. 5-15).

God's Plan Calls for Christian Workers to Share Their Needs

The disciples were instructed to inquire who in the city was worthy of God's blessing (Matt. 10:11). Apparently they were to go to one of those families and request hospitality. The implication is that God was going to bless the home that provided hospitality because of the disciples' presence. But the disciples had to be bold to the point of actually asking for lodging.

In his letter to the Romans, Paul clearly states that he expects fellow Christians to help him on his way to Spain to preach the gospel (Rom. 15:24). There appears to be no hesitation in making this statement: "I plan to do so when I go to Spain. I hope to visit you while passing through and to have you assist me on my journey there, after I have enjoyed your company for a while."

Paul makes another direct request for financial help from a church in 2 Corinthians 1:15-16: "Because I was confident of this, I planned to visit you first so that you might benefit twice. I planned to visit you on my way to Macedonia and to come back to you from Macedonia, and then to have you send me on my way to Judea."

In the Old Testament, Elijah was bold to ask for the last bit of food a widow had. The request was based on the fact that Elijah trusted God to reward the woman's faith. The result was God's provision of Elijah's need and His great blessing on the woman and her son.

> *The word of the Lord came to [Elijah]: "Go at once to Zarephath of Sidon and stay there. I have commanded a widow in that place to supply you with food." So he went to Zarephath. When he came to the town gate, a widow was there gathering sticks. He called to her and asked, "Would you bring me a little water in a jar so I may have a drink?" As she was going to get it, he called, "And bring me, please, a piece of bread."*
>
> *"As surely as the Lord your God lives," she replied, "I don't have any bread—only a handful of flour in a jar and a little oil in a jug. I am gathering a few sticks to take home and make a meal for myself and my son, that we may eat it—and die."*
>
> *Elijah said to her, "Don't be afraid. Go home and do as you have said. But first make a small cake of bread for me from what you have and bring it to me, and then make something for yourself and your son. For this is what the Lord, the God of Israel, says: 'The jar of flour will not be used up and the jug of oil will not run dry until the day the Lord gives rain on the land.'"*
>
> *She went away and did as Elijah had told her. So there was food every day for Elijah and for the woman and her family. For the jar of flour was not used up and the jug of oil did not run dry, in keeping with the word of the Lord spoken by Elijah. (1 Kings 17:8-16)*

And in Nehemiah 2:1-8, Nehemiah made a request of the king of Babylon. Note three things about Nehemiah's request in the following passage:

1. Nehemiah prayed before he asked.

2. Nehemiah asked specifically.

3. Nehemiah thought carefully about what he needed to ask.

In the month of Nisan in the twentieth year of King Artaxerxes, when wine was brought for him, I took the wine and gave it to the king. I had not been sad in his presence before; so the king asked me, "Why does your face look so sad when you are not ill? This can be nothing but sadness of heart."

I was very much afraid, but I said to the king, "May the king live forever! Why should my face not look sad when the city where my fathers are buried lies in ruins, and its gates have been destroyed by fire?"

The king said to me, "What is it you want?"

Then I prayed to the God of heaven, and I answered the king, "If it pleases the king and if your servant has found favor in his sight, let him send me to the city in Judah where my fathers are buried so that I can rebuild it."

Then the king, with the queen sitting beside him, asked me, "How long will your journey take, and when will you get back?" It pleased the king to send me; so I set a time.

I also said to him, "If it pleases the king, may I have letters to the governors of Trans-Euphrates, so that they will provide me safe-conduct until I arrive in Judah? And may I have a letter to Asaph, keeper of the king's forest, so he will give me timber to make beams for the gates of the citadel by the temple and for the city wall and for the residence I will occupy?" And because the gracious hand of my God was upon me, the king granted my requests.

SIM makes the following statement regarding raising support.

If the Lord has called you into full-time Christian ministry, it is His plan that you be supported by other Christians except in unusual cases. It is His plan, not just yours or the mission's.

Support raising is a ministry. It is not begging people for money. Rather, it is an opportunity for you to share your vision and that of SIM. People must be challenged to have a part in the Great Commission through you.

Support raising provides opportunity for blessing to those who give to you. And God gives them credit for your fruit.

Not that I am looking for a gift, but I am looking for what may be credited to your account. I have received full payment and even more; I am amply supplied, now that I have received from Epaphroditus the gifts you sent. They are a

> *fragrant offering, an acceptable sacrifice,*
> *pleasing to God. And my God will meet all your*
> *needs according to his glorious riches in Christ*
> *Jesus. (Phil. 4:17-19)*

For the sake of the gospel, it is appropriate to share our specific needs with those capable of helping us. Thus, support raising systems do not detract from trusting God as the source of the supply of your need.[3]

Clearly Scripture is not silent about finances. Through the centuries, God has supplied His people's needs through others. And you can be confident that He has promised to supply your every need as well (Phil. 4:19).

That raises more questions: Do we tell people our needs? Do we ask for support? Or do we wait in full faith that God will direct others to meet our needs without our revealing those needs? We will address these questions in the next chapter as we study the convictions of God's men of faith.

1. *Read the following verses compiled by the Navigators on biblical fund raising. Write principles or observations about support raising from each verse.*

Self Guided Training

Exodus 25:1-2; 35:4-5 *People give because they want to. They had to be told or invited.*

Numbers 8:14; 18:21-24 *Those who ask for/extend the invitation belong to the Lord; He will provide for them w/tithes*

Deuteronomy 14:27; 16:17 *People must give - that is the only source of provision - people*

1 Samuel 9:7-8 *No gift is insignificant, all are sacrificial.*

1 Kings 17:1-16 *God can provide supernaturally & will @ first then he will make you ask others; ask for all you need, expect it*

Nehemiah 2:1-8; 13:14 *Ask from where you have served; ask for connections, & letters recommending you.*

Proverbs 30:7-9 *Ask of God; know the condition of your heart 2-ward $; be content w/ needs being satisfied if you can't handle riches*

Self Guided Training

Matthew 10:5-15; 11:18-19 *Ask God's people, serve God's people; accept hospitality; bless others who give*

Luke 8:1-3; 10:1-8; 16:10-12; 21:1-4; 22:35-38 *Be a good steward plan ahead, bless, accept God's provision thru hospitality*

John 12:3-8 *the $ isn't the focus → the act of giving is.*

Acts 10:2-4; 18:3-5; 20:33-35 *God will prepare people to give, Jesus is your message, be an example*

Romans 15:20-24 *Come to God's people for refreshment; focus efforts on those who haven't heard of Jesus*

2 Corinthians 1:16; 8-9; 12:13 _____

_____

Galatians 6:6 _____

_____

Philippians 4:10-20 _____

_____

1 Thessalonians 2:9 _____

_____

2 Thessalonians 3:7-9 _____

_____

1 Timothy 5:17-18; 6:17 _____

_____

2. *What is the biblical basis for the Christian worker's being supported by others? See Numbers 18:21-24; Matthew 10:5-15; Luke 8:1-3; Acts 18:3-5; 1 Corinthians 9.* *It is part of being a good steward*

_____

_____

3. *Is there a biblical basis for soliciting or making needs known? See 1 Kings 17; Matthew 10:11; Romans 15:24; 2 Corinthians 1:16.* *Yes*

_____

_____

4. *Should a Christian worker have savings accounts or investments? Proverbs 6;6-11; 13:22; Matthew 6:33; Luke 16:11; 3 John 5-8.* *Yes*

_____

_____

_____

_____

Each person should study the above passages and answer the questions for himself. Then share observations together.

Group Guided

Training

Notes

1. The American Missionary Fellowship position paper on its financial policy.
2. & 3. The rest of this chapter is adapted from SIM materials, permission granted from SIM.

Chapter 3

Andy was convinced not only that raising support was necessary and beneficial, but that the process was biblical as well. Scripture confirmed that, but now he focused on another concern. Was it right to ask for funds? Andy had talked to other missionary friends who each had his or her own perspective. To ask or not to ask? That was the question.

Bud Taylor of the Source of Light Ministries, International, says, "The problem of misunderstanding concerning 'deputation' is that much misinformation has circulated without delving into the facts. Frequently, the negative aspect has been woven into a shadowy shroud wrapped around the subject suggesting something gruesome. Deputation seems to be an area having more misconceptions, more half truths, more unnecessary complications and more oversimplification than any other area of missionary service."[1]

The following articles identify different models for raising support.

Why Not Do It Like George Mueller?[2]
by Jocl Darby

Someone asked me the other day why we did not support Book Fellowship soul-winning enterprises as George Mueller did with his orphanages—tell no one but God about the needs. This person could not have realized that this had been my heartfelt dream in the early days of the work, for I am an ardent admirer of Mueller and his great work.

How I longed to be like this man who would tell not a soul of his needs, but fed and clothed all his orphans through secret prayer. How I longed to tell about such miracles of supply to His glory! And so we tried it. We worked and waited and prayed, but the needed funds did not come in. We searched our hearts for anything that could hold back answers to prayer.

We got answers to many other matters, real miracles, but not for this cherished hope of running the work like Mueller did. Then one day we read of some early experiences of Dwight L. Moody, who has left an even more monumental work behind him than Mueller. (Many thousands of young people, still going to the mission fields of the world.)

I was shocked to learn that Moody made no bones of declaring the needs, even to slapping a Christian businessman on the back and suggesting he invest a few thousand dollars in precious souls! I shuddered (and am still far from able to use that tactic for fund raising), but who am I to say he was NOT led of God when he did it? I am sure that the businessman who responded (he's up in heaven by now) is mighty glad he did not spend it on something else.

Wrestling in prayer over this to find God's will in the matter, I was reminded of my experience of working for the Gideons. I have spent thousands of hours of volunteer work in this fine Gideon ministry, have organized many Gideon camps here in New York state, etc. How vivid is the memory of some heated discussions in the annual international conventions over the difference of opinion of fund raising ethics! Some of our finest brethren did not agree with the plan of going to any but the soundest fundamental churches for funds, and there were folks who did not even like to make the needs known publicly at all, just wanted to use the George Mueller method.

But over the years I can see the wisdom of God's leading us as Gideons into our churches annually, with the report of God's faithfulness in using the Word in a mighty way in the lives of men. Millions of church goers who had been, through ignorance, getting their only religious teaching through churches where pastors who did not preach the true Gospel (nor even believe in the verbal inspiration of its every verse) get at least one glimpse of Christian businessmen who love and believe the Word implicitly and they learn of its mighty power to change men's lives.

We came to realize, finally, that God has His own plan for every organization which He raises up, and it is up to us to find His will for our particular situation and follow it faithfully. We waited on the Lord most earnestly, yielding in every respect we knew how to do His will, giving sacrificially of our own incomes, giving our services all

*We came to realize, finally, that God has **His own plan** for every organization.*

these years without remuneration, and waiting on Him to show us how much and how little to announce the needs.

We have made our share of mistakes, but they were honest mistakes. God knew it and used them to teach us to do a better job next time. And He has *always* met the needs in His own way and His own time, using the need of finances often to teach us our most important lessons. Many thousands have been saved and hundreds of thousands of family circles have been turned into prayer circles through God's mighty use of this ministry that He raised up.

Perhaps His most important reasons for not allowing us the quiet George Mueller method was to enlist thousands to earnestly PRAY for the work. It is a fact that you pray more regularly and earnestly for the work which you yourself support. God did not want to support this work by large amounts coming miraculously from unknown sources. He wanted thousands of people praying intelligently, each one becoming truly one of us in sacrifice and prayer for precious souls. We feel sure we followed His leading and will learn all His reasons up there.

God Is Faithful

I personally have seen God work miracles as I've asked individuals to be involved financially in our ministry. And I have seen God expand our ministry. In 1972, we started Inner City Impact on a sidewalk. We had no staff, no place to meet, and, obviously, no finances. But we had a vision. Our desire was to bring hope to inner city children, and I will never forget the first financial gifts we received from friends who believed in us and in our vision.

Soon we found an old union hall that miraculously became available for no charge. When God provided us with our own facility two years later, the challenge increased. We had to raise funds to pay the mortgage, insurance, remodeling costs, and maintenance. It was my job to challenge people to give.

And God was faithful. People caught the vision, and new contacts were made. When God put them in front of me, I had to muster up the courage to invite them to be a part of the financial solution to our needs. The ministry has continued to grow until today we have three youth centers in Chicago. Every year God supplies hundreds of thousands of dollars to support the workers, facility, and program costs.

You, too, have needs, and God will send you chosen servants who are capable of giving; they need to be asked, and that is where you fit in.

A Miraculous Way to Function[3]
SIM

I always have been intrigued with the way Christian organizations handle the subject of money. Some ignore it altogether, as though to mention it is evil; others talk about it ad infinitum.

Let me share some principles that govern SIM's use of money.

The first is that *we look to God for the provision of our needs.* Nothing could be more biblical than that. Over the years, missions that are funded this way have become known as "faith missions." The Concise Dictionary of the Christian World Mission defines "faith mission" as "the term generally applied to nondenominational and interdenominational foreign mission agencies, whose governing concept is to look to God alone for financial support." SIM qualifies.

It's a miraculous way to function. There is no human guarantee, no assurance of funds from any source. But God supplies. Each year we make financial forecasts—budgets, if you please—because we want to be good stewards of the funds brought to us, but undergirding every SIM financial statement is the proviso "as the Lord provides." Yet we are experiencing a gift income which meets our needs of approximately $30,000 every day of the year.

That leads to the second principle: *we inform God's people of the needs.* We do this because God meets these needs through His people. People are the channels He has ordained for accomplishing this purpose. We believe, however, that God's people should avoid "glandular giving"—meeting needs because of their emotional appeal. For this reason, we provide factual information and background so stewards will be able to evaluate adequately the needs presented.

We are taught in the Scriptures to avoid being tossed about by "the sleight of men, and cunning craftiness" (Eph. 4:14). That applies primarily to doctrinal truths, but it applies to financial stewardship. God expects His children to use their minds as well as their emotions in the matter of stewardship.

Some people question the element of faith in this second principle. They feel that it negates the first principle. We disagree. The principle, in fact, is very biblical. There is no question in my mind, by the way, that God led such giants of the faith as Hudson Taylor and George Mueller in their decisions that God alone should be informed of their needs. Certainly that is not inconsistent with Scripture, but clearly it is not the only biblical way of exercising faith.

The apostle Paul was open and explicit in what he had to say about stewardship. With no embarrassment whatsoever, he sent Titus and another brother to Corinth to collect funds for the needy in Jerusalem. Nothing could be more forthright than the appeal he made and the instructions he gave in 2 Corinthians, chapters eight and nine.

Even so, if there is any problem that troubles missionaries—especially new ones—it's the matter of discussing funds. Humanly speaking, it's a very difficult thing to do, particularly in regard to one's own support needs.

Why do they have this problem? In large measure, it seems to me, it is both a cultural and a spiritual issue. Our whole system of giving has been based on a concept of charity that elevates the donor and downgrades the recipient. The giver is the gracious benefactor, and the receiver is the unfortunate victim of circumstances. That is *not* the Christian way of looking at stewardship. Biblical principles are diametrically opposed to such an attitude. Paul puts it this way:

> *Our desire is not that others might be relieved, while you are hard pressed, but that there might be equality. At the present time your plenty will supply what they need, so that in turn, their plenty will supply what you need. (2 Cor. 8:13-15)*

Christian people *need* to give. It is part of the Christian experience, rooted in the fact that God gives to us. Paul elaborates on that by saying:

> *This service which you perform is not only supplying the needs of God's people, but is also overflowing in many expressions of thanks to God. Because of the service by which you have proved yourselves, men will praise God for the obedience that accompanies your confession of the gospel of Christ, and for the generosity in sharing with them and with everyone else. And in their prayers for you, their hearts will go out to you, because of the surpassing grace God has given to you.*
> *(2 Cor. 8:12-13)*

SIM is not looking merely for contributors—people who are not truly involved with us. We are looking for stewards who understand what biblical giving is. This is why we feel free to come to you, to encourage you to be part of what God is doing in Africa.

The final principle zeros in on our responsibility as the recipient of funds provided by God's stewards: *integrity in their use.* It is vitally important that we use such money as wisely and effectively as we know how. We join with Paul in saying: "We want to avoid criticism of the way we administer this liberal gift, for we are taking pains to do what is right, not only in the eyes of the Lord, but also in the eyes of men" (2 Cor. 8:20-21).

We are accountable to God, of course, but we also make ourselves accountable to those of you who participate with us. We will use what God channels in the direction of SIM in the way that is pleasing to Him, and which is fully consistent with your designation of gifts.

What does all this add up to? The fact that we are workers together, sharing our varied resources—including money—to achieve goals for God in Africa. In doing this, we explain the needs: (1) missionaries require support; (2) operating funds are needs; (3) projects such as our seminary relocation in Nigeria demand huge sums.

Can we cope with it all? Yes. Despite rising inflation? Yes. The secret lies in all of us together looking to God in faith, a lesson well taught by Rowland Bingham, founder and first general director of SIM, who loved to sing:

> Faith, mighty faith, the promise sees,
> And looks to God alone;
> Laughs at impossibilities,
> And cries, "It shall be done!"

Are Missionaries Beggars?[4]
by Don W. Hillis

"How to be sure of the will of God" has been replaced as the number one problem of Christian young people who are thinking of missions. The big hangup now is money. They object to begging for support.

David Howard says, "It is the complaint I hear with more consistency than any other. Again and again students say to me, 'I believe I am as committed to the Lord as I can be. I want to serve Jesus Christ. I am perfectly willing to go overseas and serve the Lord, but this business of going around and drumming up my support, I cannot buy it. I will not buy it!' " Howard describes the attitude of many potential missionary candidates in these words. "You've got yourself set with all your affluence, and now I come to you on my hands and knees and ask you to support me."

Horace Fenton, Jr., of Latin American Mission, says, "If raising his own support by making contacts with churches and individuals bugs a potential candidate today, we ought to be concerned about it. If our system is right, we ought to be able to prove it to these young people. If it's wrong, we ought to be seeking a better way to do the Lord's work."

Tom Watson, Jr., adds, "They are right . . . it is a problem. There is something underlying the method that tends to degrade the candidate . . . it does support an economic double standard . . . the missionary does have experiences where he laughs because he doesn't want to cry. Maybe there is a better way. If so, what is it?" Fortunately, it is possible to be both sympathetic and scriptural toward the problem. And just as fortunately, the scriptures are far from silent on this issue.

23

In the Old Testament economy those who served the Lord and His people (the priests, Levites, and prophets) lived off the tithes and offerings of the people. And there was a definite relationship between Israel's faithfulness in giving and God's blessing upon the nation. The prophet Malachi accused Israel of robbing God in relation to tithes and offerings. He then promised that God would open "the windows of heaven" to those who would be faithful in the matter of giving (Mal. 3:8-10).

Jesus, who so easily could have turned stones into bread and who multiplied loaves and fishes, lived off the gifts of His friends during His public ministry. Then He pulled the economy rug out from under the feet of those He called into His service. He insisted that the fishermen should leave their fishing, the tax collector his tax collecting, and the tent maker his tent making. When Jesus sent out the seventy "into every city and place," He commanded them to "carry neither purse, nor script, nor shoes." They were to accept the hospitality of those who would open their homes, "eating and drinking such things as they give: for the laborer is worthy of his hire" (Luke 10:4-7).

Whether it involves the preacher in America or the missionary overseas, the Lord has ordained that those who "preach the gospel should live off the gospel" (1 Cor. 9:14). And is a pastor expecting his people to support him any different from an apostle (missionary) expecting churches to support him?

As far as I can discover, Paul only apologized once to the Corinthian believers—for failing to insist that they should share his support. He assured them that this is a way they could prove the sincerity of their love for God. He warned them of the danger of sowing sparingly and encouraged them with the reward of sowing bountifully. He assured them that God is able to make all grace abound toward them in this matter of sacrificial giving. He reminded them that God loves a cheerful giver.

Paul used as illustrations (1) the Macedonian believers who gave out of their deep poverty; (2) Christ who gave up the riches of heaven; and (3) the Father's willingness to give His indescribable Gift to us. Though Paul as a missionary had learned how to be abased and to abound, how to be full and how to hunger, he rebuked those who were careless about giving to the Lord's servants and commended those who were faithful. The missionary does not accept the gifts of God's people as handouts for his personal well-being. He is a representative of God's work. That work does not go on unless God's servants do it, and they cannot do it without support.

"But," says the missionary candidate, "I have no objection to being supported by God's people. My objection is to begging for support."

To this there are three answers. The candidate may join any one of many denominational mission boards in which he has no responsibility to raise support. This is appealing and doubtless has some valid advantages, but it also has some weaknesses. Or he may join a faith mission which uses a pooled support program. In such a situation, he is expected to trust the Lord to supply his needs. However, he goes to the field whether or not he received sufficient support. God has honored this method and some splendid and effective work is being carried on by missions that use it. Another answer is to take a new look at some values found in raising one's support. Several of today's largest and fastest growing missionary organizations use this system. And the personalized support program is a basic contributing factor in their growth.

Deep, personal relationships between the Christian worker and his home church do much to promote a long-time interest in both giving and intercession. And without the intercession of many friends, the battle can be lost. Furthermore, any deep sense of God's leading should be accompanied by the confidence that when He guides, He also provides. Raising one's support is a challenge to faith.

Dr. Fenton shares this wise counsel with missionary candidates: "See yourself not as a huckster of your own services or as a promoter of your own support, but as one who has had firsthand contact with God—and who, therefore, has something to share with others. See your mission to the churches not as a money-raising junket, but as a further fulfillment of the great commission; you are going because of a divine call—to share with others what you know of Jesus Christ." When the missionary candidate sees raising of his support as an opportunity to prove his faith, to inform fellow Christians of God's work, to inspire them to invest in things of eternal consequence, and to encourage them to pray for him and for the work of the Lord, then his deputation is no longer a mountain but a ministry. He probably will even find himself making new personal friendships that will be of rich spiritual benefit to him, to his friends, and to his work. There is no substitute for friends who really care.

"After all pious platitudes have been swept away," says Fenton, "you will need the friendship, the prayers, and the deep interest of God's people more than you need your monthly support. And a period of prefield deputation may be the means God will use to give you a wider circle of praying friends than you presently have." Paul appears to have counted the Philippian church as his home church. He had no sooner left the newly-found church at Philippi (Acts 16) than they sent financial aid to him. He received at least two "support checks" from them during his two weeks in Thessalonica (Phil. 4:16). Later when writing from Rome he said, "I rejoiced in the Lord greatly that now at the last your care of me hath flourished again" (Phil. 4:10). These believers never lost their interest in supporting Paul, but apparently there were times when they had no way of getting money to him.

Though this great missionary was willing to go without the necessities of life, he told the Philippian believers they had done well in supplying his financial needs. He obviously felt other churches should have done the same, and thus have fruit that would abound to their account (Phil. 4:14-17).

The common denominator in the accounts of Elijah accepting the hospitality of the widow of Zarephath, Elisha rooming with the Shunammite family, Jesus eating in the home of Mary and Martha, and Paul enjoying the gracious hospitality of Philemon is that of giving and receiving. Though the recipients did not take the kindness of the givers for granted, neither did they apologize for being on the receiving end. In each of these cases, a warm personal relationship was built up between the giver and receiver.

There are hundreds of missionaries whose testimonies

corroborate that of TEAM's missionary Bessie Degerman as she says, "I would not exchange the faith-expanding experiences I had watching the Lord supply my needs for going to Japan for anything. It has been one of the highlights of my missionary experience."

Are missionaries beggars? I guess the answer really depends upon one's perspective of God's work and interpretation of His Word.

For some missionary candidates it is convenient to hold to a position of not asking for support. Asking for support is not a conviction at all, but something they want to avoid at all cost. International Teams provides the following article in their support handbook for consideration.

Why Do We Lean to the "Faith Principle"?[5]

1. It sounds spiritual.

> *But seek first His kingdom and His righteousness; and all these things shall be added to you. (Matt. 6:34, NAS)[6]*

> *But if God so arrays the grass of the field, which is alive today and tomorrow is thrown into the furnace, will He not much more do so for you, O men of little faith? (Matt. 6:30, NAS)*

> *And my God shall supply every need of yours according to His riches in glory in Christ Jesus. (Phil. 4:19, NAS)*

2. It sounds logical. Such a philosophy is compatible with our minds as well as our hearts.

3. It makes us feel good. We like to be thought of as individuals who have matured in Christ.

4. It shields us from being accused of promotional and self seeking ends, or of being unspiritual.

5. It provides a good "out" if failure occurs. We continue to be above reproach because we can say, "It was God's will."

For some missionary candidates it is convenient to hold to a position of not asking for support.

27

6. It avoids our having to "raise funds" from the Christian public, something we may not excel in and feel uncomfortable doing.

7. It avoids associating ourselves with secular and often unethical practices. Nobody wants to be thought of as a used car salesman.

8. It avoids having to ask someone to "take care of us."

- Paternalistic connotations.
- We were raised to "pull our own weight."
- Nobody wants to be a "beggar."
- American work ethic: success.
- Associations with "the Dole," i.e., welfare.
- Personal pride (all of the above).

9. It avoids the threat that we may be doing the work of the Spirit for Him.

10. People will not feel pressured by our presentation—we don't like to push anyone.

11. It avoids the possibility of our facing rejection of our cause, method, or selves.

12. It appeals to us to seek confirmation of God's leading into missions by successfully raising our support by faith.

13. It is assumed that if we can't trust God with our finances while on support discovery, how will we trust Him on the field?

A key to successful support raising is for you to determine what God wants *you* to do. It may not be the easy way or the most comfortable; spiritual growth happens when we are forced beyond our resources to lean on the Lord for courage and wisdom.

As you personally develop a support raising plan that fits into God's purpose for you, He will enable you with confidence to proceed.

Dr. George Sweeting, chancellor of Moody Bible Institute, summarizes the three approaches to fund raising in the following article.

Blessed Are the Money-Raisers[7]
by George and Donald Sweeting

"Blessed are the money raisers, for in heaven they shall stand next to the martyrs." So spoke D. L. Moody almost a century ago, as both the foremost evangelist and fund-raiser of his day.

The church and para-church organizations exist not to make profit, but to help people in worship, discipleship, missions, and the physical needs of life. In Old Testament times, Israel had the Lord to make its solicitations, requiring a tithe of one's firstfruits. Ever since, however, things have become complicated. We face several possibilities.

One approach to fund raising is to engage in prayer alone. In other words, no information and no solicitation.

A second option is to pray earnestly and also to provide information, but to refrain from any direct solicitation.

A third method is to provide full information, coupled with varying degrees of solicitation. The extremes of this third approach to religious fund raising are Pope Clement VI, who in 1344 threatened excommunication to those who failed to give, and Oral Roberts, who claimed in 1987 that God would take his life if a specific amount of money was not received by a certain date.

The issues of fund raising face most Christian ministries, and the way they are dealt with has made an impact on the thinking of American—40 percent are reported to think that only some or very little of religious fund raising is honest. Nevertheless, in 1985, more than $37 billion was collected in America for religious causes.

The present sophistication of religious fund raising, complete with computers and direct mail, is a recent phenomenon. One hundred years ago, fund raising was primarily a one-man operation.

Picture evangelist Moody just home in Northfield, Mass., after an extended campaign in one of the major cities of the world. Appeal letters were typed for him by the hundreds and occasional thousands (there were no photocopy machines). Moody preferred to sign them rather than have his signature stamped. He would spread the letters throughout his office on the floor and furniture so that the ink would dry. This is how Moody's son Paul remembers his father at home.

These mass mailings were unique for the religious organizations of his day. Yet they proved to be an effective technique for Moody that others would soon imitate.

For some time there has been a debate in evangelical circles: In guiding a ministry, should one be aggressive in raising funds, or is it more biblical or spiritual to pray and wait upon God to act? That debate continues, but it appears for good or ill that aggressiveness has prevailed.

D. L. Moody probably had something to do with the outcome of this controversy. This is especially clear when we compare Moody to some of his contemporaries, like George Mueller and Hudson Taylor.

Mueller is the evangelical's prototype of the passivist. He worked in Bristol, England, and founded homes for orphans. His biographies are filled with stories of faith about how no one knew a particular need but God alone, and right when the need was most urgent, the money for which Mueller prayed miraculously came in.

Regarding solicitation, Mueller said, "It is not enough to obtain means for the work of God, but that these means should be obtained in God's way. To ask unbelievers for means is not God's way. To press even believers to give is not God's way; but the duty and privilege of being allowed to contribute to the work of God should be pointed out, and this should be followed up with earnest prayer, believing prayer, and will result in the desired end."

For Mueller, the key was in waiting on God for the annual 25,000 pounds to provide for his 200 children. He spent time praying that would ordinarily go to fund raising. He wanted to prove God's faithfulness. Once he even withheld the annual statement of his ministry, lest someone consider its information to be an appeal.

But Mueller did inform the public about the progress of his work and gave account of how funds were used. All he asked of his supporters was to pray for God's provision. There was minimal information and no solicitation.

Hudson Taylor, founder of the China Inland Mission, was burdened to recruit workers for the missionary enterprise. Like Mueller, he made no appeals for money. He wanted to sustain the work by prayer alone. In an attitude that is almost incomprehensible in our own day, Taylor wanted to avoid diverting funds from older benevolent societies. Subscription lists were out.

"The apostolic plan," he said, "was not to raise ways and means but to go and do the work, trusting His promise who said, 'Seek ye first the kingdom of God and His righteousness and all these things shall be added unto you.' " God's work done in God's way would not lack God's supply.

For Taylor this meant that if there was a need, he would pray and tell others about the need. He was considerably more aggressive than Mueller in announcing his needs. For example, in the "First Occasional Paper" of the mission in 1866, the exact amount of the needs was specified in print.

So in practice, Taylor went a step further than Mueller. He believed and practiced "full information, but no solicitation."

Moody differed from these two evangelical giants, and he knew it. Biographer John Pollock writes that Moody had a slight suspicion of such enterprises run in faith without an appeal. He did not understand them. For him, faith meant doing something as well as believing something. He said, "I show my faith when I go to men and state to them the needs of the Lord's work and ask them to give to it." And ask he did.

If Mueller practiced minimal information and no solicitation, and if Taylor stood for full information and no solicitation, then Moody stood for both full information and, for the most part, full solicitation. This aggressiveness was startling to some in the evangelical orbit. In fact, the Moody Bible Institute today differs from its founder by sharing full information coupled with gentle, faithful solicitation.

Moody differed from Mueller and Taylor for two significant reasons. First, Moody was a former businessman.

In his doctoral dissertation, James Howell Smith recites an incident from Moody's life in 1898. A successful Wall Street businessman was asked, "How is it that while you and other men like you are all but inaccessible, fenced in by closed doors and polite but immovable secretaries, D. L. Moody can see you at any time?" The financier replied, "He is one of us."

By inclination and by training, Moody was a businessman. At an early age he left home and moved to Boston where he entered business by selling shoes in his uncle's shoe store. Selling excited Moody. While other salesmen waited for people to come to them, Moody went into the streets after customers. Early on, he set a goal of earning $100,000.

As Moody gained experience, his wages and the opportunities at the Boston shoe store seemed too small. Moody decided to move to Chicago, where another uncle lived. In 1856, this uncle helped him secure a job in a Chicago shoe store. Within a short time of his arrival in the prairie city, Moody's goal of $100,000 seemed within reach.

At this point, however, Moody also began to take his Christian faith seriously. He divided his time between business and church work. John V. Farwell, a successful Christian businessman, became Moody's model.

The only problem was that Moody's outreach to the children of Chicago through Sunday school work had so captured his attention that he sensed God's calling him to devote all his talent and time to the work. And what was his primary talent? Salesmanship—a persuasive practical mindedness, backed up by abundant energy and an earnest heart.

Moody, then, was a businessman who entered the gospel ministry. He thus brought a whole different mind-set to the work of evangelism.

Second, **Moody differed from his contemporaries with respect to fund raising because he believed it was highly honorable to raise money for a worthy cause.** To beg even a nickel for oneself was dishonorable, but to beg a fortune for others was of great significance.

For what projects did Moody solicit funds? First there was his Sunday school class, which grew to more than a thousand. Encouraged by Farwell, Moody raised $20,000 in 1863 to erect a building for his school, which would later become the Illinois Street Church (forerunner to the Moody Memorial Church). Moody was twenty-seven at the time.

Next, Moody took interest in the YMCA, which was primarily an evangelistic association. Moody raised money for three Chicago YMCA halls, both before and after the Chicago fire. He also raised money for chapters outside of Illinois.

In raising money, Moody sometimes issued stock certificates stating that the owners had bought shares in the enterprise and could claim their dividends from rent charged to non-YMCA organizations that used the building's facilities. Moody, though, wanted investors to know that their stock would bring a larger return in heaven than on earth.

One of his most noted donors to the YMCA work was Cyrus H. McCormick, founder of International Harvester. Moody asked McCormick for $25,000, saying, "More depends on your decision than on that of any other man. Your name will help us through.

The public will think if you take hold of it, it must succeed!"

Moody also raised a great deal of money to initiate his schools, two in Northfield and the Bible Institute in Chicago. From 1879 until his death twenty years later, his total solicitations for the three schools amounted to about $1.8 million. The schools, the YMCA, and the church were causes worthy of his aggressive abilities.

On his British tours, Moody raised funds for buildings sponsored by the YMCA and other Christian groups in Liverpool, Manchester, Dundee, Edinburgh, Glasgow, Belfast, and Dublin. Henry Drummond, who worked with Moody in Britain, said, "There is scarcely a great city in England where he has not left behind some visible memorial." And again, "His progress, though great in Britain and Ireland . . . is marked today by halls, churches, institutes and other buildings which owe their existence directly to his influence."

Of Moody's skills, Drummond said, "Mr. Moody is the most magnificent beggar Great Britain has ever known. He will talk over a millionaire in less time than it takes other men to apologize for intruding upon his time. His gift of extracting money amounts to genius."

Moody's secret, said Lyman Abbott, another friend, was his **"artless faith that all money belongs to the Lord, and that it can be had for the Lord's work if one goes about in the right way to get it."**

This attitude of honorable money raising was also seen in Moody's wariness to avoid situations that would appear to make him gain personally. He even gave the royalties on his books to needy causes. As Drummond said, "His appeals are wholly for others . . . for places in which he would never set foot again; for causes in which he had no great personal stake."

James H. Smith concludes, "Moody, who raised hundreds of thousands of dollars for other causes, considered it wise publicly and personally to avoid the temptation of financial situations in which he himself might capitalize." Smith adds, "Philanthropists trusted Moody to recommend donations that would go completely to the charities rather than accumulate in his accounts."

Moody's associate and successor, R. A. Torrey, said of him, "Millions of dollars passed into Mr. Moody's hands, but they passed through; they did not stick to his fingers."

Apparently for these reasons, then, Moody took a more

aggressive approach to fund raising. He was trained to be aggressive, and he believed he could use that training to serve the Lord. He dressed like a businessman, talked like a businessman, thought like a businessman, and raised money like a businessman. But his business was world evangelization.

Other than winning and discipling souls, Moody earnestly believed that the best thing he could do for anyone was to help him lay up some of his treasures in heaven.

As I review Sweeting's article I am reminded that there are three components to support raising: prayer, information, and solicitation.

Using those three components, we can identify at least three models that have been used over the years.

Model 1: George Mueller—prayer alone.

Model 2: Hudson Taylor—prayer and information, but no solicitation.

Model 3: D. L. Moody—prayer, information, and solicitation.

The question is, which model for support raising does Scripture teach exclusively?

Answer: There is no one model. There is no right model and no wrong model.

Self Guided Training

1. *How did George Mueller and D. L. Moody differ in their approaches to raising funds? Whose approach is right?*

(see Box) they are both right

2. *Think about this quotation from Joel Darby's article: "How I longed to be like [George Mueller] who would tell not a soul of his needs, but fed and clothed all his orphans through secret prayer. . . . We worked and waited and prayed, but the needed funds did not come in." How do you think the writer felt at that point? How would you feel?* like a failure, that maybe he had misunderstood his calling.

3. *Joel Darby said, "We came to realize, finally, that God has His own plan for every organization which He raises up, and it is up to us to find His will for our particular situation and follow it faithfully." Can God have more than one plan for raising support?* Yes

4. *What did you learn from reading "Why Not Do It Like George Mueller?"* God will meet needs His way & His timing & use finances to teach us deeper lessons.

Self Guided Training

5. *What three principles are described in "A Miraculous Way to Function"?* 1. look 2 God 2. tell God's people of the needs 3. exercise integrity in using the $

6. *Do we lack faith if we share our needs with people? Why or why not?* No, we are operating IN faith by asking.

7. *Hudson Taylor and George Mueller believed that God alone should be informed of their needs. Certainly that is not inconsistent with Scripture, but is it the only biblical way of exercising faith?* No

8. *How did Paul reveal his financial needs to other Christians?* Telling them, writing letters

9. *Do you think Christians need to give? Why or why not?* Yes → it grows their faith & expresses their love for God

10. *In the Old Testament, how did the priests depend upon the people to meet their needs?* tithe

11. *How was Jesus dependent upon His friends for His needs?* $, hospitality

12. *Were the seventy dependent upon other Christians for their needs?* Yes

13. *Is it biblical for you to depend upon people to meet your needs?* Yes.

14. *David Howard hears the complaint, "I am perfectly willing to go overseas and serve the Lord, but this business of going around and drumming up my support, I cannot buy it. I will not buy it!" Why do young people make such statements? What advice would you give that person? Have you ever felt like that? What is your attitude today on this issue?*

We are taught Not to beg → my attitude is changing.

15. *Which of the following statements best represents your feelings on support raising?*
I view support raising as a huge problem, a mountain that seems insurmountable.
I view support raising as an opportunity, a challenge to see God at work. I am looking at support as a ministry.

Self Guided Training

16. *How, specifically, can raising support be a ministry? Give several examples.* _____
_____
_____
_____
_____
_____

17. *In the article "Are Missionaries Beggars?" the writer talks about a warm personal relationship being built between the giver and receiver. That is illustrated between Paul and Philemon, and in missions it would be reflected between the missionary and his faithful supporter.*

Identify a close friend who could potentially serve as a supporter. In several paragraphs describe the type of relationship you would like to have with him/her regarding raising support. How would the relationship you just described differ from the relationship based on begging for support?

Becka _____

_____ Not Close _____

_____

18. *Are missionaries beggars?* No
Why or why not? They are Connectors between God's people & God's blessing
_____

19. *Review each of International Team's thirteen statements.*

20. *Identify the missionary personality related to Model 1, and describe that philosophy of support.* _____
_____ pg 34 ____

21. *Identify the missionary personality related to Model 2, and describe that philosophy of support.* _p 34_

_____

_____

22. *Identify the missionary personality related to Model 3, and describe that philosophy of support._ _p 34_

_____

_____

23. *Consider the following statements as they relate to a support raising philosophy:*

> *There is no <u>one model</u>.*
> *There is no <u>right model</u>.*
> *There is no <u>wrong model</u>.*

Do you agree? Why or not? _Yes_

_____

_____

_____

24. *Moody differed from his contemporaries with respect to fund raising because he believed it was highly honorable to raise money for a worthy cause. Do you believe raising support for your ministry is an honorable cause?* _Hmmm_

_____

_____

_____

Group Guided Training

1. *Split into small groups and discuss the above questions.*

2. *The author of the SIM article indicates that Christian people need to give. It is part of the Christian experience, rooted in the fact that God gives to us. Do you agree? Why or why not?*

3. *The author of the SIM article indicates that SIM is looking not merely for contributors but for stewards. What is the difference?*

4. *Break the group into three small groups.*

The first group takes the position of George Mueller and defends his philosophy. The second group takes the position of Hudson Taylor and defends his philosophy. The third group takes the position of D. L. Moody and defends his philosophy. Give the small groups time to meet as a group to prepare. Then each group makes a presentation to the entire group.

Notes

1. Bud Taylor, *Taking the P.U. Out of Deputation* (self-compiled pamphlet).
2. Joel Darby, deceased.
3. SIM, Africa Now, Nov./Dec. 1976, p. 15.
4. Don W. Hillis, retired missionary of The Evangelical Alliance Mission.
5. These thirteen points are adapted from *Personal Support Raising Manual* (Prospect Heights, Ill.: International Teams, n.d.), 9-10.
6. *New American Standard.*
7. George and Donald Sweeting, from *Lessons from the Life of Moody* (Chicago: Moody Press, 1989).

Chapter 4

As Andy explored the various philosophies of support raising, he realized that there was not one biblical model that was right for everyone. He would have to develop his own personal philosophy.

A smile spread across his face as he realized the challenge before him. No matter what direction he took to secure his support, he would be stepping out in faith. There was no guarantee that his support would come in, except that a faithful God was leading him.

As you examine this issue, you will also have a variety of thoughts regarding support raising. Even Overseas Missionary Fellowship (OMF), which by policy does not authorize its missionaries to solicit funds, recognizes that that is not the only biblical model. In an article titled "OMF Finance—Why We Don't Appeal for Money" David Dougherty explains:

> The OMF policy is deceptive because nonsolicitation is made to seem a scriptural requirement.
> Candidates may be attracted to OMF because of the nonsolicitation policy for the wrong reason:
> A reluctance to 'raise support' rather than a desire to trust the Lord for provision.
> We do not view non-solicitation as a Biblical requirement for us or for any other organization. We do not consider it necessarily to be the best policy. It is simply God's way for us.[1]

Although there is no one biblical model and no guarantees, support raising does require a walk by faith. Let's look again at SIM's philosophy statement. SIM provides this sample philosophy statement.

The first principle is that we look to God for the provision of our needs. It's a miraculous way to function. There is no human guarantee, no assurance of funds from any source, but God supplies. Each year we make financial forecasts—budgets—because we want to be good stewards of the funds brought to us. But undergirding every financial projection is the proviso "as the Lord provides."

The second principle is forthrightly informing God's people of the needs. We do this because God meets these needs through His people. People are the channels He has ordained for accomplishing this purpose.

The apostle Paul was open and explicit in what he had to say about stewardship. With no embarrassment whatsoever, he sent Titus and another brother to Corinth to collect funds for the needy in Jerusalem. Nothing could be more forthright than the appeal he made and the instructions he gave in 2 Corinthians, chapters eight and nine.

The third principle is that we recognize Christian people need to give. It is part of the Christian experience, rooted in the fact that God gives to us.

The final principle, integrity in the use of money, zeros in on our responsibility as the recipient of funds provided by God's stewards. It is vitally important that we use such money as wisely and effectively as we know how.[2]

Workers Together

What does that add up to? The fact that we are workers together, sharing our various resources—including money—to achieve goals for God.

Support raising can be viewed as a three-pronged relationship:

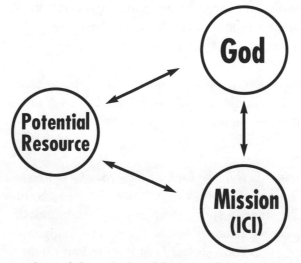

Each member of the relationship has a job description or boundary in which he or she must operate.

Mission

The mission ought to communicate its needs (financial, personal, or other) to both the potential resource and the Lord.

Potential Resource

As a member of the worldwide body of Christ, the individual ought to be willing to listen and be made aware of the needs of the mission. He or she then ought to pray, sincerely asking God if it is His will to respond to a particular need.

God

God is responsible for providing for the mission according to His will and for burdening individual members of the body of Christ to respond to the mission as He sees fit.

While growing up in the home of missionaries, I watched my mom and dad live lives of faith. When we were having a home built, we prayed for every phase, and we watched God provide.

As a student at Moody Bible Institute, I listened intently as missionaries told their personal stories of faith, and I was intrigued. To fulfill mission class assignments, I read missionary biographies that described the excitement of living by faith rather than by sight. Yet I had never taken great steps of faith of my own. When we began the ministry of Inner City Impact, I was confronted with the question of how to raise funds. I watched, studied, questioned, and hammered out what became my personal philosophy of raising support. God led our family and our mission this way, but He may lead you to operate differently. For more than twenty years all of our needs have been met, and the entire ministry is debt free.

ICI, realizing the realities of communication, will seek to communicate needs in the most personal yet practical way possible.

ICI recognizes that it is far more effective to share financial, personal, or prayer needs person-to-person, rather than depending only on impersonal tools.

ICI will share its needs in a positive and enthusiastic manner.

ICI, wherever possible and practical, will seek to identify separate audiences and develop varying strategies to each.

How Inner City Impact Communicates Its Needs

43

ICI will seek to do a balanced job of reporting tastefully both successes and failures.

Development and programming will always be conducted with quality methods and materials.

The Mission will meet the standards held by the Evangelical Council of Financial Accountability, of which we are a charter member.

As a ministry, we expect to develop appropriate strategies based on the philosophies spelled out previously, but in all cases we will turn to the Lord in prayer and expect Him to work above and beyond our strategy.

Since people give to people, ICI will seek the support of its staff, board, donors, and other interested friends of the ministry to help reach new Potential Resources. ICI will, in all cases, operate in an honest and credible way.

As stated earlier, there is no one biblical model for fund raising and, therefore, ICI recognizes differing views, but for the sake of unity, all staff must be willing to live with this philosophy.

We are accountable to God, and we also make ourselves accountable to those who participate with us. We will use what God channels in the direction of ICI in a way that is pleasing to Him and is fully consistent with the designation of gifts.

1. *Identify on the continuum below which fund-raising model you subscribe to.*

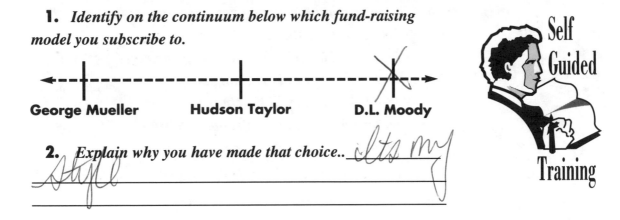

George Mueller   **Hudson Taylor**   **D.L. Moody**

Self Guided Training

2. *Explain why you have made that choice..* _Its my style_

3. *Which statement best describes how you made your choice:* **Based on Biblical conviction:** _X_
Based on Convenience: _____

4. *"Some missionary candidates may hide behind George Mueller out of convenience, not necessarily out of conviction." Do you agree with that statement? Explain.* _Yes they are fearful and too lazy_

5. *"All support raising philosophies ultimately are dependent upon God and faith in His ability to meet your need." Rewrite that statement in your own words, showing that you understand its underlying meaning._ The ability lees w/ God not man or his methods_

Self Guided Training

6. *In preparation for writing your personal philosophy of support raising, answer the following questions.*

- *Are there biblical commands or principles that I need to heed in raising support?*
- *What principles will I include in my philosophy statement of support raising?*
- *What principles will I exclude in my philosophy statement of support raising?*

yes
— integrity
— serve
— focus on Jesus
+ ask, seek, knock

_____

_____

_____

7. *Write your philosophy statement of support raising.*

_____

_____

_____

Group Guided Training

Each person should prepare the questions under Self-Guided Training. Break into small groups, and discuss.

Notes

1. David Dougherty, "OMF Finance: Why We Don't Appeal for Money," *East Asia's Millions,* November/December 1989, 281.
2. SIM.

Chapter 5

Andy was amazed by the number of negative thoughts that surfaced as he thought about raising his support. As he read and talked with others, he became excited about starting the process. Yet, some nagging fears lingered.

The following article by Curtis Kregness of New Life Editions helped Andy put some issues into perspective.

The "Enemy" of Deputation Was Me[1]

Deputation. I've never had a real secure feeling about that word. It sounds too much like deportation or deprivation.

To those within missionary circles— especially eager candidates—the word "deputation" can strike fear into otherwise stout hearts. To those outside the church, it is an unknown term.

I know that "a rose by any other name would smell as sweet," but couldn't we try to come up with some alternative to "deputation"? How about "expectation," or "anticipation," or "initiation"?

At the beginning of my missionary career, deputation loomed menacingly ahead, a big question mark that was to dominate my life for the next two years. After talking with veteran missionaries, I sometimes got the feeling that it was some kind of initiation rite into a sacred order. If you passed the test and survived deputation, you had what it took to "make it" on the mission field. It was like a type of boot camp, which toughened one's mettle for more difficult times to come. The veterans I talked with tended to remember the positive aspects and gloss over the rocky portions.

I entered deputation with some apprehension, not really knowing what to expect, but realizing that I was in for a long, arduous climb. I was convinced of one thing— that God was going to have to take up the slack in many places, because I felt very inadequate for a public relations-type ministry, especially when it often centered on myself.

Deputation, as we all know, is a ministry. "But what does that mean?" I thought. I know it's supposed to mean that the missionary appointee is intended to be a blessing to the host church(es). We are supposed to inspire, challenge, encourage, inform, exhort, edify, and otherwise impress our constituents. But as I climbed further up the mountain, I discovered that someone had not told me the complete story. God was using the deputation experience to minister to me. At each new bend in the trail, I realized some new lesson that God was teaching me, which went far beyond the fund-raising and prayer-raising function of deputation.

Lesson 1 *Increased confidence in God and self.*

In an area like public speaking, where I felt most inadequate, God took away my fears and allowed me to express my thoughts in a coherent, understandable fashion. At one point, I even received an encouraging compliment on my presentation from a 3-M marketing expert. I was amazed.

Lesson 2 *Flexibility.*

I learned what it meant that an appointee was supposed to be able to "preach, pray, or die at a moment's notice." For instance, being asked at the last minute to teach not just the high school class (your original assignment) but the entire adult department for Sunday school. Or being called on to "give a word of testimony" at a meeting in which you thought you would be able simply to sit back and relax for once. "Good missionary training," the veterans said. I agreed, begrudgingly.

Lesson 3 *Patience.*

The hardest thing about deputation is waiting. Waiting for news of support; waiting for the next meeting; waiting for your printed prayer letter from the home office; waiting for a visa; waiting for letters from the field; waiting for your car to get repaired. Somehow, God managed to teach me patience through all that waiting.

Lesson 4 *Learning to meet new people.*

I never did enjoy meeting total strangers. I'm still not sure I do. But it certainly has gotten easier. Because that's what deputation is all about: going to places you've never been, to meet people you've never met before, to talking about something you've never experienced before. But now, I have a few less strangers in our denominational family and a few more friends. The concept of the universal family of God became vividly real to me. Many times, I felt that I received more encouragement from my host family than I was ever able to give them in return.

Lesson 5 *Learning to be an alien.*

The missionary appointee on deputation is an alien. First, he becomes an alien to his home community because he is never around to attend church or other social functions. He can accept no steady responsibilities in his church or community because he can never be sure when he will be called out of town for a meeting. Second, the missionary appointee is an alien wherever he goes to speak. Of course, he makes a few good friends in most churches, but those relationships quickly are cut off when he must hop in his car and head to the next meeting.

A feeling of rootlessness begins to pervade the appointee's life. This was one of the most difficult aspects of deputation for me. Once, when I returned from a five-week deputation circuit out of town, I discovered that many things had transpired in my church and among my circle of friends while I was absent. I felt "out of it." But suddenly my shock was doubled when I realized that this was exactly the same situation I would face when I returned to the U.S. after four years overseas—only the feeling of alienation would be compounded many times over. Thanks for warning me in advance, Lord.

Lesson 6 *Reevaluation of my missionary call.*

Missionaries often convey the idea that they "have it all together" in terms of their call to missions. Don't believe it. The doubts creep in occasionally. But when one is continually forced to express his call to those who have never experienced God's convictions regarding overseas service, some heavy thinking is required. A mere whim of the moment cannot be sustained through months of deputation. There must be solid study of God's word and strength of inner purpose to face the ups and downs of this period. I decided that my commitment to God and His work in the world could not be based on my feelings or my knowledge of the future, but on His faithfulness alone. That is the only type of "missionary call" that will last.

The comic strip character named "Pogo" once uttered this piece of wisdom: "We have met the enemy and he is us!" My deputation experience verified that often we are our own worst enemies.

One of the first psychological challenges I had to face was the change from "9 to 5" type work to the sporadic schedule of the self-employed appointee. I discovered that this amounted to periods of frenzied preparation, followed by long hours behind the wheel of my car, followed by intense segments of emotional drainage (speaking or meeting people), followed by repetition of the whole process. I longed for the predictability of a 40-hour work week.

Self-discipline, I discovered, was the key. Spare moments between meetings could be used productively for letter-writing, reading, physical exercise, washing the car, etc. There wasn't much time left for goofing off.

The second inner barrier I faced was a growing sense of nonproductivity. In my previous job, I usually had something tangible to show for my day's work—an article edited, a brochure designed, a news story roughed out, a slide show script written. But as an appointee, I soon realized that most of my "product" was intangible. I didn't like that feeling. How could I monitor my progress? How did I know whether I was succeeding or failing? What did I tell someone when they asked me what I did for a living?

During these times I gained consolation by remembering verses like 1 Corinthians 15:58 and Hebrews 12:11. God was developing my character. Now that's a product. And though I couldn't see it, I knew that God was developing a sense of responsibility and accountability in the lives of those who heard my missionary challenge.

Then there was still another barrier—that mystical

change to missionary status and the subtle consequences that accompany it. Was it my imagination, or were people treating me differently? It was as if they were carefully putting me in a different pigeonhole.

"Oh, so you're a missionary. I see. That's nice. Uh . . . very interesting. Well, best of luck. See you later."

I could almost see the wall of nonunderstanding develop in some cases.

"A missionary? Wow, I'd better be careful what I say. This guy must have a hotline to God. Why would anyone want to throw his life away like that? I feel sorry for him—all that suffering and persecution he will go through in some out-of-the-way corner of the world."

"We have met the enemy and he is us."

Oh, the monologue was never spoken, but I could read it between the lines. And it made me uncomfortable. I didn't want to be different; I wanted to be a plain old ordinary sinner, just like everybody else. I didn't want a hotline to God. Sometimes I wasn't even sure if I knew His number. And most of all, I didn't want to be pitied. That turned my stomach.

Maybe it was that word—"missionary." Maybe it should be thrown out along with "deputation." Too many barnacles clinging to it. Too many false impressions. Maybe I should start calling myself a cross-cultural literature specialist. No, that's too cumbersome. Anyway, it's not my fault that people don't understand what a missionary really is—or is it?

Finally, there was that painful wondering if you can truly be someone's friend without them thinking that the ulterior motive for the friendship was some kind of financial support for your missionary enterprise. This one really hurt. I decided that most of the problem was in my own head. Any problem that someone else had was strictly a misunderstanding of what a missionary is and how God provides his support. Nevertheless, the thought still surfaces every once in a while, and must be dealt with. "We have met the enemy and he is us."

As Kregness concludes his article he wonders if one can truly be someone's friend without their thinking that the ulterior motive for the friendship is to gain financial support for the missionary enterprise.

A number of years ago I met a man who had great financial capability. At a rally promoting Inner City Impact he placed a card in the offering plate indicating a pledge of several thousand dollars. He also indicated that he wanted to meet with me.

I set up an appointment with him, and we had an enjoyable time. He paid his initial pledge, and future gifts came our way. But soon he hit hard times. In a time of recession, his company suffered losses and eventually went bankrupt. From a financial standpoint he had little to offer me or our ministry, but something dynamic had taken place. We had developed a true friendship. We prayed together, cried together, and rejoiced together. Support had come to mean more than money.

Are You Your Number One Enemy?

Many missionaries are their own worst problem when it comes to raising support. It all begins with their attitude and vision (or lack of vision) for support.

As you read these chapters, you may be struggling. You have heard stories about support raising, and part of you doesn't want to do it. The other part knows that God wants you to do it.

Don't allow yourself to be your own worst enemy of support raising. Instead, allow the process of seeking support to strengthen you. Permit God to go before you and open the doors to meet with people who will become partners in your ministry for Him.

Self Guided Training

1. *Write down your own fears about raising support.* _rejection, making a mistake w/$_

_____

_____

2. *Flexibility is a key ingredient in raising support. In which three areas in your life will it be the hardest for you to be flexible as you raise support?* _____

_____

_____

3. *Patience is another key ingredient. On a grading scale of A-F (with A being very patient and F being very impatient), how would you rate yourself in the area of patience? Take time to pray that the Lord will give you patience as you raise support.* A

4. *What difficulties and fears do you experience when you meet strangers? How do you handle them?* = do it scared.
→ Small talk Challenge
→ fear = Judgments

5. *The missionary appointee on deputation is an alien. First, he becomes an alien to his home community.*
- *How will you handle that?*
- *How will your spouse handle that?*
- *Your children?*
- *How do your parents feel about your support raising responsibilities?*
- *How do your parents feel about your requesting funds from other relatives?*

**Group
Guided**

Training

1. *Discuss the questions above as they relate to each individual's situation.*

2. *Choose one of the following methods for continued study on this topic.*

- *Ask one individual to present the topic of the number one enemy and its ramifications to the entire group.*
- *Ask a veteran missionary to share his or her experience in this area.*
- *Invite a missionary panel to discuss the subject.*
- *Break into small groups to talk about the problems one encounters in raising support.*

Note

1. Curtis Kregness, *Evangelical Missions Quarterly* for "The Enemy of Deputation Was Me," October 1986.

Chapter 6

As Andy reflected on the process of raising support, he thought of the word *ministry*. He was realizing that support raising really is a ministry.

He reflected on the stories he had heard about the problems of raising support. Many people seemed to make a distinction between support raising and missionary service. It was as if they didn't enter the ministry until they got past the support raising and onto the field. But Andy determined in his heart that his ministry would begin as he raised his support.

What Is Support Raising?

On the surface, some people identify support raising as prayer letters, church meetings, mission committees, fear, and rejection. Bud Taylor of Source of Light Ministries, International suggests that for such people deputation "is thought of as a period of 'endurement' instead of 'endearment.' "[1]

But support raising is far more than a mechanical process. Taylor continues, "Your ultimate ministry is to serve others—right? Then let serving others become the basic motive of your entire missionary career *beginning now*! . . . Let your missionary service begin here at home, where you have no language barriers, no culture shock, no government restrictions."[2]

In *The Ministry of Deputation*, Dr. Earnest Gambrell says, "When God calls a young person or young couple to missionary service, are they in the ministry? Absolutely! They are in the ministry. Do they then leave the ministry for one, two, or more years to do deputation? Absurd! Right? Of course it is. They are in the ministry from the first moment they surrendered to the call of God. They do not leave the ministry to do deputation; they simply conduct their deputation 'as a ministry.' "[3]

Gambrell explains further that Webster's dictionary defines deputation as "a group of persons or one person appointed to represent others." Deputation is exactly that—presenting the need of a third party.

In Nehemiah 1 and 2, the prophet Nehemiah had been in captivity at the hands of the Babylonian empire for several years. One day, some men came from Judah, and Nehemiah asked them about those who were left behind during the Captivity and about

Let your missionary service begin here at home.

55

Jerusalem. Their response, "Those who survived the exile . . . are in great trouble and disgrace. The wall of Jerusalem is broken down, and its gates have been burned with fire" (v. 3), caused Nehemiah to weep and mourn. His heart was burdened for Jerusalem and the people.

We can draw an analogy from that text regarding a missionary on deputation. Somewhere between 1:4 and chapter 2, it is safe to say that God burdened Nehemiah's heart to go and do something about the condition of Jerusalem and the people.

Chapter 2 tells us that Nehemiah was the king's cupbearer. He had not been sad in the king's presence before, but his heart was so burdened that it showed in his countenance. Let me add here that if a missionary's heart is truly burdened, it will show, and others will notice it. If a missionary does not have a burden, he ought to stay home!

The king saw Nehemiah's expression and asked, "Why does your face look so sad . . . ? This can be nothing but sadness of heart" (2:2).

Nehemiah responded, "Why should my face not look sad, when the city where my fathers are buried lies in ruins, and its gates have been destroyed by fire?" (v. 3). Nehemiah was presenting the need of a third party.

When a missionary is invited to a church, he is asked to share his call, his field, and his burden. He presents not himself but the needs of a third party. He is there not simply to preach to the church, but to share with the church the needs of the people of the field to which he is going. His goal is to make them aware of the people's spiritual need, the spiritual darkness that blinds them, and the burden that God has placed on his heart to reach them.

I do not know of a greater opportunity to minister than deputation. World missions—the spreading of the gospel to those who have never been reached—is not only the closest thing to the heart of God but is indeed the heart of God. It is the one thing that is sure to touch the hearts of God's people. Yet it is one of the least discussed subjects in the pulpits of the United States today. A missionary on deputation has a unique opportunity to minister to the church. Furthermore, a missionary on deputation may have the opportunity to speak in some churches where an evangelist would give his "eye-teeth" to preach![4]

African Evangelical Fellowship reminds us of the following principles relative to deputation as ministry.

1. Be convinced that raising a support team is ministry. Deputation to raise support can be one of the most satisfying experiences you have ever had. Helping other Christians to see how they can become a part of a "team" that will make an impact for Christ is a special privilege. You are not going out in your name to do your thing. You are going in the name of Jesus Christ to do the work to which He has called His church. You are giving God's people an opportunity to fulfill their stewardship responsibilities. Someone told me that the missionary becomes the link between the church and the lost world and any Christian worth his salt would want to encourage that kind of person.

2. Be convinced that you are helping the church's ministry. Frankly, the pastor in the local church can be a bottleneck when it comes to talking about money. Some pastors are threatened when someone comes in and wants to challenge the people. You must be convinced that you are not there just to get "support," but that missions is a joint venture involving the missionary and the "support team"—the church. When individual members begin to get involved in personal support, prayer will usually follow and interest in missions picks up.[5]

Also there are two types of ministry: (1) Our public ministry, i.e., church meetings, and (2) our personal ministry, i.e., caring for people. The public ministry is great for public relations, but our personal ministry is critical for funding.

How Can the Missionary Minister to Donors?

Your goal is to do things for donors that friends do—send birthday, anniversary, get-well, and holiday cards.

Send regular ministry reports and pictures, including updated pictures of your family.

Send thank you notes for financial gifts. A missionary from one country wrote notes on the back of wrappers from local products. It added culture and interest to an ordinary letter.

Send small gifts of appreciation from your area, such as unique items, recipes, crafts, even a care package of local food products. The gift could be as simple as a ribbon bookmark or some foreign coins.

As you become better acquainted with your donors, keep notes about their special interests. If they are collectors, add items to their collections, such as stamps, postcards, or knickknacks.

Invite your donors to visit you on the field. When they come, look for ways to involve them in ministry with you.

Let your donors know that you are praying for them. Share your prayer requests, and follow up the requests they share with you by asking for updates. Seek ways to introduce your donors to one another.

Show an interest in the children of your supporters. If they have a report to do on your country, send information or items for them to incorporate. Tell interesting stories about children from your country. Link up children with pen pals from your country.

Help your supporters become better acquainted with your country. Share pictures, maps, data sheets, or the country's flag.

When you are on home leave, entertain and be hospitable even if you don't feel settled. Be involved in your local church, and find short-term places to serve.

How Can the Support Team Minister to the Missionary?

Supporters can show their friendship and care for the missionary in a variety of ways, such as writing letters, sending holiday cards, phoning, or sending local newspaper and magazine subscriptions. A fun thing is to put a party in a box and send everything they would need to celebrate a birthday or holiday.

Consider what you would like to receive if you lived away from home—a sports video, cassettes of favorite music or the pastor's sermon, bulletins and news from church, an up-to-date church directory, prayer letters of other missionaries supported by the home church, special foods or other items not available where the missionary lives, fashion catalogs, or books.

A church member who is a printer could offer to print the missionary's prayer letters. An accountant could help do his or her taxes or provide financial expertise. A computer whiz could help the missionary load and learn to use his computer. A media expert could help produce a video or multimedia presentation. And almost anybody can baby-sit, give a food shower, take the missionary shopping, help build shelves in the temporary home, build crates, help pack, loan a car, or help locate a car or housing or schooling.

Encourage the interest of others at church by addressing envelopes to the missionary and making them available for church members to write letters. Or bring a cassette recorder to a gathering, and ask everyone to speak to the missionary. Take your vacation, and visit the missionary. Design a bulletin board showing the missionary's work.

The ideas are endless. A concerned donor should sit down with his family and others interested in missions and brainstorm about practical ways to show love and care for the missionary. Concerned individuals will discover many additional ways to care for the missionary.

Bud Taylor adds that the call is to a person not a field of service. God used Moses (Ex. 4:10-12) and Isaiah (Jer. 1:6-8). We can be confident that God is performing His work in and through us (Phil. 1:6), and when the going gets tough we cling to God's promises. In short, Taylor reminds us, "We are out to prove that deputation is a privilege, not a persecution."[6]

Support raising will stretch us, but Mark McCloskey of Campus Crusade encourages, "God permits you to have just the right amount of adversity and blessing."[7]

In these first six chapters, I have laid the groundwork to stimulate your thinking on support. First, your positive attitude toward support raising makes the difference between your enjoying it as a ministry and viewing it as a necessary evil. The latter attitude is deadly.

Second, your positive attitude makes a difference in your ability to attract support. Everyone appreciates positive people; their energy is inspiring. Their smiles and optimistic outlook on life is attractive. God's people like to be around positive servants.

Third, your positive attitude brings joy to your heavenly Father. He is honored when we want to accomplish His work with a joyful heart.

It's your choice. You are the only person who can decide to have a positive attitude toward your support raising. Your mission can't legislate it. Your church missions committee cannot require it. Your donors can't force it on you.

What will be your attitude? The basis for thinking positively is whether you choose for support raising to be your ministry and do everything in your power to be God's best representative in the exciting days ahead.

Chuck Swindoll provides us these thoughts about attitude:

" The longer I live the more I realize the impact of attitude on life. Attitude, to me, is more important than facts.

It is more important than the past, than education, than money, than circumstances, than failures, than successes, than what other people think or say or do. It is more important than appearance, giftedness, or skill. It will make or break a company... a church... a home.

The remarkable thing is we have a choice every day regarding the attitude we will embrace for that day. We cannot change our past... we cannot change the fact that people will act in a certain way. We cannot change the inevitable. The only thing we can do is play on the one string we have, and that is our attitude...

I am convinced that life is 10% what happens to me and 90% how I react to it. And so it is with you... we are in charge of our Attitudes."[8]

Self Guided Training

1. *Write a paragraph or two expressing your current feelings on raising support. Be specific, and don't be afraid to share your real feelings and concerns.*

I'm excited to prepare the system & materials required to raise support. although a little apprehensive about actually asking for $ → no problem asking for participation or help in other areas.

It needs to be done & can be part of the business of IT.

2. *What is the worst scenario that could happen as you seek to raise your support? Write it out.* _They would say no & tell me why what i'm doing is wrong, dumb, not important_

3. *List five major obstacles that could prevent you from raising support.* _1. fear of rejection 2. lack of integrity 3. no one left to ask 4. procrastination 5. no preparation_

4. *What steps will you take to handle each of those obstacles?*

_____

_____

5. *What attitude do you want to have regarding support raising?* _positive, energized, excited_

_____

6. *What will you do specifically to maintain a positive attitude and view support raising as a ministry?* _review scripture_

_____

7. *What attitudes could cause you to lose sight of support being a ministry? Have you prayed about them?* _____

_____

8. *On a scale of 1 to 10 describe your attitude toward support prior to reading this book, with a 10 being a very positive attitude.* _4_____

9. *On a scale of 1 to 10 describe your current attitude toward support, with a 10 being a very positive attitude._ _8_____

Group Guided Training

This is the last chance for your group to lay the groundwork for a positive attitude toward support. Each person should complete the Self-Guided Training and turn it in. Your follow-up will be critical. If questions are answered honestly, you will need to counsel some in your group.

In the near future, these individuals will be involved in the process of raising support. Unless they handle attitude problems now, their problems will be magnified in the midst of support raising. That could cause the process to drag on for a long time with limited success. Now is the time to uncover fears, concerns, and negative attitudes, and address them.

Notes

1. Bud Taylor, *Taking the P.U. Out of Deputation* (Self-compiled pamphlet).
2. Ibid.
3. Ernest Gambrell, *The Ministry of Deputation* (Memphis: Fundamental Baptist World-wide, 1987), from chapter 1.
4. Ibid.
5. Donald B. Patterson, "Raising Support: Practical Tips in God's Economy," African Evangelical Fellowship.
6. Taylor, *Taking the P.U. Out of Deputation.*
7. Mark McCloskey, (Campus Crusade, Staff Training Tape, July 1991).
8. Creeds to Live By, (©1993, Celebrating Excellence Inc., Lombard, IL).

Cultivating the Necessary Skills for Support Raising

Chapter 7

Andy talked with as many missionaries and mission contacts as he could about the process of support raising. He was hoping that someone would give him a sure-fire plan of action.

The more people he spoke with, however, the more confused he became. Some talked about newsletters as if they had to be major productions. Others talked about booking meetings. And others talked about making prayer cards and slide presentations. As the list grew, Andy's frustration increased. Where should he start? How would all those ideas fit together?

I need to come up with a plan, Andy said to himself. *I don't want to just go through the motions. I need to know that what I plan to do is the right thing to do at the right time. And I don't want just any plan. I need a plan that will be the most effective strategy for me.*

Principles of Support Raising

If you are raising your financial support, you must develop a general strategy. A plan to discover supporters starts with the conviction that God already has chosen those people to support you. As you follow His direction, He will lead you to people who are willing and able to support you. Consider two principles, the first of which is divided into four parts.

Principle 1

> **People give to people.**
> **People give to people they know.**
> **People give to people they know and trust.**
> **People give to people they know, trust,**
>   **and care for.**

This principle can be summed up in one word: *relationships*.

Because support raising is developing relationships among caring people, start by contacting people the Lord has already brought across your path—people who know you, trust you, and care about you. In later chapters you will learn how to broaden your contacts by meeting new people in a logical and natural way.

Principle 2

> **The key to raising support successfully is to contact people you know in the most personal and practical way possible.**

What does that mean? The *Harvard Business Review* did a study of forms of communication and ranked them according to effectiveness in the following order.

1. One-on-one
2. Small group discussion
3. Large group discussion
4. Telephone
5. Handwritten letter
6. Typed letter
7. Mass letter
8. Newsletter
9. Brochure
10. News item
11. Advertisement
12. Handout

If you measured existing support systems against those two principles, to what extent would you say they employ the most effective methods of communicating their message?

I see two major problems in some of our mission support systems, and they violate our two principles. The first problem is what I call the shotgun approach. Eager to raise support, the missionary rushes off in every direction. He or she looks through the yellow pages for any church that might have an evangelical tag. Such prospective missionaries wander into the unknown and waste time, energy, and money contacting people who don't know them, trust them, or have a deep concern for them. That violates Principle 1.

The second problem is developing a strategy of support raising around the impersonal approach. New missionaries spend bulks of time and finances on mass mailings to long lists of people. When letters don't produce the results they desire, those prospective missionaries get discouraged, give up, and never make it to the mission field.

I promote letter writing, but notice that according to the *Harvard Business Review* survey, mail is ranked the fifth, sixth, and seventh best ways of communicating. Letters alone will not get the job done. The primary focus for communicating your support needs must be one-on-one visits.

Only 7 percent of communication is done through words. Ninety-three percent comes through expression, gestures, tone, and body language. A personal, face-to-face meeting provides access to the "total" communication.

Below is an actual case study of a missionary who tried to secure his support. His heart, no doubt, was in the right place, but note the high utilization of impersonal tools.

Case Study 1

Deputation was started August 1986 after candidate school. Full-time deputation began August 1, 1988, and ended August 21, 1989.

Miles driven: 33,000

Money spent on direct expenses (not personal): $8,530

Monthly financial support needed: $2,000

• Churches contacted	164
• Information packs sent	155
• Pastoral meetings set up after sending information packs	58
• Meetings resulting from the 58 pastoral meetings	26 with 9 pledging support
• Meetings from phone calls after sending packs	8 with 2 pledging support
• Meetings from churches of family	6 with 5 pledging support
• Meetings from churches calling me	3 with 0 pledging support

- Churches spoken in   43
- Churches spoken in twice   4
- Churches spoke in many times   4
- Bible study   1
- Total meetings   51+

Of 42 churches, 16 provided financial support. Those 16 churches represent 75 percent of the monthly support. The remaining 25 percent is made up of individuals.

Note the strong focus on meetings, rather than individuals. Also note the length of time needed to raise full support, the miles driven, and the cost.

Now read the following case study of a woman whose focus was on individuals.

Case Study 2

Name: Julie

June 28-29:   1-1/2 days of training

June 30:   Began support raising while maintaining a full-time job of forty hours a week

August 2:   Gave boss six weeks' notice. Took one week vacation for camp while still raising support.

September 6: $1,597 raised in monthly pledged support and $5,628 in special gifts

September 16: Began full-time ministry

Julie raised her full support in ten weeks through the following process. First, she sent 106 initial letters to her friends. Then she called forty-one of those people and scheduled thirty-eight appointments.

The results of the thirty-eight appointments were as follows: thirty-one people met with her and agreed to support her. One person agreed to support her later. One person's company gave a substantial gift, and he chose not to give personally. Another group promised a gift, and she met with four people who did not give; she will pursue them when additional funds are necessary.

In addition to those thirty-eight appointments, Julie saw the Lord bring in additional gifts when four people who did not even receive a letter heard about her through the grapevine or met her for the first time and decided to support her. Five people who only received a letter (and no follow-up phone call) responded in a positive way to support her. Three people who received letters and follow-up calls, but had no appointments, agreed to support her. Finally, she received a call from someone who had only heard of her and that person agreed to support her at $100 per month.

Note the brief time (ten weeks), the focus on individuals, the good response she had in setting up appointments (thirty-eight out of forty-one), and how God worked above her strategy to bring in additional gifts.

So in our high tech age, Christians need to be high touch when it comes to raising support. Visiting with prospective donors is cost effective and time effective, and can result in a highly committed support team.

In our high tech age, Christians need to be high touch.

Where Do You Go from Here?

When you start to raise your support, apply the first principle. Systematically identify whom you will target—the people who already know, trust, and care about you. Those individuals become your audience and the foundation on which you will build your support strategy. Then apply principle 2; systematically meet one-on-one with as many people as is possible and practical. By doing so, you will:

- Renew and strengthen friendships with former acquaintances.
- Meet interesting people and make new friends.
- Share your excitement for the Christian ministry and God's work in and through you.
- Develop your ministry and communication skills.
- Be challenged to invite people to support you financially, in prayer, and in other ways.
- Experience new adventures in faith.

In addition, the people you contact will benefit. They will:

- Meet a dedicated missionary.
- Gain a new perspective on how God is working.
- Become supporters of a cutting edge ministry.
- Experience God's blessing as they give of their finances and energy.

Even John the Apostle when he penned the epistle of 2 John back in 90 A.D. understood the importance of meeting with people face to face. He writes in 2 John 1:12, "I have much to write to you, but I do not want to use paper and ink. Instead, I hope to visit you and talk with you face to face, so that our joy may be complete."

If I could give you only one word of advice, it would be to see people personally. There is no question but that the strategy of going to people personally will work for you as you follow these twelve steps.

"I hope to visit you and talk with you face to face,"

(2 John 1:12)

Step 1: Begin with My Home Church
Step 2: Determine to Whom I Will Go for Support
Step 3: Record and Catalog Prospects
Step 4: Mail the First Prayer Letter
Step 5: Make Appointments
Step 6: Conduct the Visit
Step 7: Track Support
Step 8: Say Thank You
Step 9: Conduct a Letter/Phone Strategy
Step 10: Expand Contacts
Step 11: Cultivate Support
Step 12: Resolicit for Support

Some potential missionaries will have trouble starting with Step 1 because they do not have a "home church." If that is your situation, you should skip Step 1 and proceed to Step 2. But for those who have a home church, starting with Step 1 is vital.

The following chapters provide specific steps to take as you raise support. Pray for an open heart, and let's begin the journey of support raising that will bring these benefits.

1. *Fill in the blanks of Principle 1.*

People give to ___people___ .

People give to ___people___ *they* ___know___ .

People give to ___people___ *they* ___know___ *and* ___trust___ .

People give to ___people___ *they* ___know___ *and* ___trust___

and they ___care___ *for.*

Self Guided Training

2. *Principle 2 says, "The key to raising support successfully is to contact people you know in the most personal and practical way possible." What does it mean to contact people in the most personal way? What does it mean to contact them in the most practical way?* ___People you know___

___focused not shot-gun___

_____

If you were to witness to someone, what kind of personal communication would you use to share the gospel? Do you think that support raising requires the same level of personal communication? Why or why not? ___Yes → where___

___their $ is, is where their ♥ is___

_____

3. *Interview a veteran missionary concerning his or her experiences in support raising. Ask the following questions:*

Approximately what date did you officially begin active support raising?_____

Approximately what date did you reach your support goal?

_____

How much did you have to raise?_____

How long did it take you?_____

How many churches did you contact?_____

At how many churches did you speak?_____

How many churches took on your support?_____

How much did they commit in support?_____

What percentage was that of the total support raised?_____

Self Guided Training

*How many individuals did you contact?*_____

*How did you contact them?*_____

_____

*How many individuals took on your support?*_____

*What percentage was that of the total support raised?*_____

*What did you enjoy most about support raising?*_____

_____

What methods of support raising were most successful for you?

_____

_____

*What things do you wish you had done differently?*_____

_____

_____

*When the interview is completed, think about that missionary's process of support raising. Write a summary statement to evaluate the process he or she followed.*_____

_____

_____

_____

Group Guided Training

1. *Each group member should complete the questions above.*

2. *Break into groups, and discuss your analysis of the missionary you interviewed. Each group should share its findings with the rest.*

Chapter 8

Andy was beginning to understand that the focus of raising support is not on financial benefits alone. And it isn't a shot in the dark to unknown people, either. It is the process of developing relationships. He would invite friends to join him in his journey toward mission service.

But Andy still had questions and fears. How would he develop these relationships? Why should his friends support him? What if he couldn't raise enough support? How should he begin?

Because he respected his pastor as both a friend and spiritual leader, Andy decided that he would begin by calling him to set up an appointment.

In 1972 when I began my missionary service, I was eager to share the gospel with the children of Humboldt Park in Chicago's inner city. But I didn't know who would pay the expenses of the work. As my wife, Sandy, and I looked forward to starting a family, we wondered, *Where will our support come from?*

We didn't have an organized mission board backing us. Beginning a new ministry by faith, we were confident that God would supply. The Holy Spirit prodded us: "This is the way; walk in it." So seeking spiritual direction, I began by calling my pastor.

Contacting the Pastor

It is a great thrill for a pastor to know that a member of his congregation is obeying God's call to missions. So set a time to meet with your senior pastor, and share your burden for the ministry to which the Lord has called you.

My pastor was a visionary—a man who spoke quickly, listened intently, and offered timely advice. As I think back, I'm sure I saw the glimmer in his eye as he began to catch my burden for ministering in the inner city. I know he saw the glimmer in mine.

Understanding my tremendous financial needs, he promised to help. He suggested ways in which I could share my vision with the church, and eventually the church voted to carry part of

Step 1: Begin with My Home Church

12 Step System

our support. In addition, many individuals from my home church have contributed money, time, and energy to our ministry.

By contacting your pastor first, you recognize him as a spiritual leader and seek his approval before proceeding to enlist support from your church. You will benefit from his counsel now and in the days ahead. You need to have him on your team.

Because the pastor is a key decision maker, he can recommend you as a missionary candidate to the mission committee and to potential supporters both inside and outside your church. He can explain the church's missionary program to you and suggest ways that you can minister in the church. His approval—or disapproval—of your plans for missionary service will help determine how much support the church will give. So begin to build a working relationship with your pastor.

Because church organizational structures are different, be flexible. In large churches, it may be impossible to meet with the senior pastor. Instead, you will be referred to an associate minister. He may have the authority to recommend you to the missions committee and to others. And once you have met with the associate minister, the door may be opened to meeting with the senior pastor later.

Let me give you a hint as you plan to contact your pastor. I never call pastors on Mondays because many pastors take Mondays off. And I don't call on Wednesdays because they are preparing for the midweek service. I never call Fridays because many pastors are completing the preparation for their Sunday sermons. By calling on a Tuesday or Thursday, I am most likely to gain the pastor's attention and be able to set a time to meet with him.

Goals for Meeting with the Pastor

What you accomplish in your meeting with the pastor depends on how thoroughly you prepare for it. You should have five goals for your meeting.

Your first goal is to articulate how God led you into missions and your burden and vision for missions. I suggest that you write out your statement and rehearse it. Stand in front of a mirror, or sit in a comfortable chair and practice your presentation. Talk enthusiastically and with conviction about what God has called you to do.

Gather literature on your mission organization, including a doctrinal statement and supporting materials. Bring them when you meet with your pastor. If he is not familiar with your organization, such printed pieces will explain the mission's operation and give him confidence concerning the organization. If time permits and the equipment is available, you may want to show a brief videotape prepared by your mission.

Your second goal is to discuss your financial need. When you are asked how much support you must raise, don't sidestep the issue. Be straightforward and state the total financial goal. Indicate what that includes—for example, outgoing expenses, transportation, shipping of personal goods, insurance, housing, equipment, and other needs. Be prepared to answer questions such as, How much support do you have pledged currently? What is your target date to leave for the field? What will be your specific assignment?

But discussing your burden and need is not enough.

Your third goal is to gain a clear understanding as to what steps you should follow to make a formal request for church support.

Ask these questions.

1. Does the church have particular mission policies or procedures of which you need to be aware?

2. Who decides which missionaries will be supported? Is it the pastor, the missions committee, or church board?

3. Who is the chairperson of that committee or board? What is his/her phone number?

4. How often does the missions committee meet? When is the next meeting?

5. Who is on that committee?

6. What qualifications are set by the committee for missionaries that the church supports?

7. What are the steps for making application to receive support from the church? Is there an application or form to be completed?

8. Does the committee designate a set amount for a single person or a married couple? If so, what is it?

9. Do you need to know about any deadlines? For example, when does the missions committee set the budget for the next year?

Because one church rarely provides the total support a missionary needs, you will also need to enlist individual supporters. For that to happen people need to meet you and catch your vision.

Your fourth goal is to identify ways to present your ministry to the church. Because the key person to opening doors of opportunity in the church is often the senior pastor, ask him for ideas on where you might minister in the church. Discuss options such as:

- **Sunday morning worship service**—giving a three- to five-minute testimony, or even the main message
- **Sunday evening worship service**—giving a three-minute message or a longer presentation
- **Sunday school**—speaking to any age level (kindergarten and above) for five to twenty minutes, or for the entire class time
- **Youth activities**—giving a five- to fifty-minute presentation
- **Potluck supper**—giving a fifteen- to sixty-minute presentation
- **Midweek service/prayer meeting**—giving a ten-to sixty-minute presentation, or leading a prayer service for world missions
- **Missions committee meeting**—presenting a ten- to sixty-minute presentation
- **Retreat, conference, camp**—giving one or more fifteen- to fifty-minute presentations
- **Vacation Bible School**—giving one or more fifteen- to fifty-minute presentations
- **Women's meetings/Bible studies/other groups**—giving a fifteen- to fifty-minute presentation

My pastor called me late one Monday evening. He explained that because he had a bad case of food poisoning, he would be unable to teach the women's Bible study the next morning. Would I do it?

I was happy for the opportunity and got up early Tuesday morning to prepare. As I wrote notes, I added illustrations from our ICI ministry.

Several days later I received a check for $500 for ICI from one woman who had been in the Bible study. Today gifts from those women continue to come for even greater amounts. They first caught the vision for our ministry at that Bible study, and they have increased their support through the years.

You must be willing—sometimes—to teach a class, help in the nursery or with the youth, or to be involved in other ways. Help in any capacity in which you can, but don't tie yourself down as you need to have flexibility to schedule other support meetings.

Your fifth goal is to ask the pastor to introduce you to additional contacts—both inside and outside your church. When a dear Christian woman lost her husband, she wanted to give some of her money to missionaries. She asked her pastor for his advice, and he recommended that she include Inner City Impact in her giving.

After receiving the first gift, I phoned to thank her and began to develop a friendship with her. Today she is deeply committed to our ministry and gives liberally every year. She also has included ICI in her will.

When you talk with your pastor, keep a pencil handy and take notes. List potential ministry opportunities and people to contact.

Contacts You May Develop Through Your Pastor

Your pastor may put you in contact with:
- a Christian businessman
- another pastor who would permit you to share your ministry in his church
- a local ministerial association through which you can meet area pastors
- various Bible study groups who would appreciate listening to your missions presentation

I continue to maintain contact with pastors of our supporting churches and invite them and their wives to special ICI events. In addition, I encourage them to bring businesspeople from their churches with them as guests.

As I review our supporters, I think of six businessmen who are regular supporters. I initially met each of them when I asked a pastor to introduce me to key businesspeople who might be able to support our ministry. As God blesses these men, they often look for additional ways to give back to the Lord.

Your Ministry to the Pastor

Your meeting with your pastor will give you opportunity to minister to him as well. Your willingness to be available and involved in the church will encourage him. As you talk together, show genuine interest in his background and family; his goals for the church and ministry; ministry areas he enjoys; his problems, frustrations, and concerns; ways that he would like to see the church grow; and ways that people are responding in the church. Affirm him and empathize with him.

Yet remember the purpose for your visit. Your focus is on seeing your support need met. So before you leave, ask him to recommend the next step for you to take in raising support in your church.

You Are a Member of a Family

Whatever the mission to which God has called you, you are not alone. You are a member of a church family. As you raise support, it should be church family members who pray for you, rejoice with you, encourage you through the discouraging times that come to every missionary candidate, and contribute financially. That kind of support comes when you have made the effort to be interested and involved in the church and its members.

In the early days of our ministry, we eagerly checked the mail each day for any envelope that might contain a financial gift. When gifts came, many were small. But they added up, and we thanked God for providing for our needs. When one couple from a former church sent a gift of several hundred dollars, we were elated. That gift made a significant difference to us and was a sign that somebody understood the ministry we were launching. It made a significant difference to families in the city, too.

Now Inner City Impact is less than an hour's drive from my home church, and various church members have assisted at our headquarters. Carpenters and electricians have donated their services; individuals have done office work, and many have been involved in our children's ministries. We've seen supporters come alive as they realize that God is working through them.

That first meeting with my pastor was more than twenty years ago. Our family has grown to include three children. The Inner City Impact ministry that began with children on a sidewalk has grown to three large centers in the Chicago area.

We've used the principles in this book to help our staff to raise their support. As the work continues to expand and the financial needs increase, God's provisions have been miraculous. But His provision doesn't come automatically. It is a result of developing relationships with people whom God has led us to contact.

Be Flexible

Because each church organizational structure is different, the suggestions in this chapter are just that—suggestions. Adjust them to your situation.

Do not be discouraged if you don't come away from the initial meeting with your pastor with a list of confirmed speaking engagements. Churches have limited speaking opportunities, and pastors may have many requests from prospective missionaries and mission organizations. Be willing to take advantage of any opportunity that your pastor offers. Thank the Lord for openings even if you cannot see how a specific engagement will help you raise support.

God will direct your ministry and provide in surprising ways in the days ahead. The key is to take specific notes when you meet with your pastor and follow up on every suggestion that he makes.

Because it is unlikely that your home church will take on your full support, meeting with your pastor is just the first of twelve steps to take in raising support. *Before proceeding with this step of meeting with the pastor, continue reading until you grasp all twelve steps and fully understand the deputation philosophy and strategy.*

Self Guided Training

1. *Write out a* <u>*presentation you will make to your pastor.*</u> *(Review the five goals discussed in this chapter.) Practice giving the presentation in front of a mirror. Do not read from your notes. Your manner should be natural and personal.* _____

_____

2. *Write down possible ways for you to share your ministry at your home church, i.e., Sunday school, worship services, or youth activities.* Small groups, networking between services, events

3. *Gather literature on your mission, including a doctrinal statement and supporting materials that will give the pastor confidence in the organization.* IT Vision

4. *Call your pastor to set up an appointment. Plan to dress neatly and arrive on time.* Pastor Sheila

5. *After your appointment, summarize your visit in writing and keep the notes in a notebook for future reference.* _____

_____

_____

Group Guided Training

1. *In preparation for your group training, complete the steps in the Self-Guided Training section above.*
2. *Role play calling the pastor for an appointment.*
3. *Discuss the options available in a typical local church for a missionary to talk about his ministry. As a group, compile a list.*
4. *Review and memorize the five goals for the initial meeting with your pastor.*
5. *Role play a presentation to a pastor by a prospective missionary using the five goals discussed in this chapter.*

Chapter 9

Andy realized that the basis for raising support was identifying his prospects. If he was to be fully supported, he would have to take a hard look at his network of friends. Categories of friends came to mind—high school, college, church, coworkers, relatives, friends of the family, neighbors— the list went on.

Looking for prospective supporters is an ongoing process, not a one-time function. In fact, as a missionary, you will never finish your list of prospects; you will always be on the lookout for new prospects.

Compile a Prospect List

You will be surprised by how quickly a prospect list grows when you group people by categories.

If you are married, you and your spouse should compile separate lists and then combine your contacts. Remember, don't leave anyone off the lists.

Church Contacts

Current church contacts. Go through your church directory name by name. Do not merely put the entire church directory on your list. Only add names of people with whom you and your family have had contact. Consider people you have met through special groups such as the missions committee, Sunday school, Bible studies, care groups, boards, and so on. Add the names of camp friends and contacts from church conferences.

Past church contacts. Think of past church staff—pastors, youth pastors, and people who have relocated and would be interested in your mission plans.

If you attended other churches in the past, carefully list the names of friends from those churches. Also, remember churches you attended while at college and during summers.

As I built my list of church contacts, I thought about a church I had attended in my grade school days. I remembered Sherril who had married a doctor and now lived in Arizona. When I contacted her, Sherril decided to support our ministry regularly.

Step 2:

Determine to Whom I Will Go for Support

12 Step System

Step 1	Begin with My Home Church
Step 2	Determine to Whom I Will Go for Support
Step 3	Record and Catalog Prospects
Step 4	Mail the First Prayer Letter
Step 5	Make Appointments
Step 6	Conduct the Visit
Step 7	Track Support
Step 8	Say Thank You
Step 9	Conduct a Letter/ Phone Strategy
Step 10	Expand Contacts
Step 11	Cultivate Support
Step 12	Resolicit for Support

81

Another couple whom I knew from my junior high years agreed to take on support when I contacted them.

Regarding support from your church contacts, you need two sources: (1) You need the church to support you, but to be satisfied with the church's official support is shortsighted; (2) you also need individuals within that church to support you.

Relatives

Not only can relatives lend their financial support; they can catch the vision of the ministry as well. I am the third generation in my family that has served Chicago's inner city since 1918.

One of my cousin's daughters also has a burden for the inner city. Representing the fourth generation, she has joined the ICI staff, with many of our relatives supporting her and our ministry.

As my wife, Sandy, was going through a list of her relatives, she thought of her cousin Jim who lived in the Indianapolis area. When Jim was in Chicago, we invited him to tour our facilities and later challenged him to give. He has been supporting the ministry monthly ever since.

On your prospect list, include the names of:
parents
brothers
sisters
grandparents
children
aunts/uncles
cousins
nieces/nephews
other relatives

Before you finish this category, talk to other family members. When I spoke with my dad, I learned that one of his cousins whom I had never met had accumulated some wealth. I made several phone calls and a visit, and eventually his family foundation decided to give an annual gift.

Neighbors

Neighbors can be a source of support. One of our neighbors heard me in a radio interview. Later he saw newspaper articles on our ministry and became a donor.

School Contacts

Review yearbooks, school directories, and class pictures.
Think about contacts you had through sports, clubs, Bible
studies, and other school activities in:
Grade school
Junior high school
High school
Junior college
College
Graduate school

Don't forget special teachers, administrators, coaches, and
other staff. Also list contacts from special Christian groups—for
example, YFC, Young Life, FCA, Navigators, Campus Crusade
for Christ, IVCF, and so on.

Keep in mind that one goal of Christian professors is to see
their students become involved in missions. When they hear that
former students are missionary candidates, they will likely lend
prayer and financial support.

Employment

Remember supervisors, owners, fellow workers, customers,
clients, vendors, professional acquaintances, salespeople, and
anyone else you had contact with during your employment.
Consider contacting your parents' employers, too. Think about
past jobs (full- and part-time) as well as your current job.

During my junior high and high school days I mowed lawns,
did yard work, and shoveled snow. Little did I realize that those
relationships from so many years ago would produce not only
donors, but members of our board.

Service Contacts

Consider the following list of professional and service
contacts.
• Barber or beautician
• Dry cleaners
• Dentist/orthodontist

- Doctors (family doctor, pediatrician, surgeon, specialists, eye doctor, and so on)
- Accountant
- Insurance agents (home, health, car, business)
- Lawyer
- Broker
- Banker
- Mechanic
- Plumber
- Baby-sitter/Preschool teachers
- Avon lady
- Printer
- Christian bookstore owner
- Contractors
- Other

Note: Check the Chamber of Commerce directories. They might jog your memory with other names.

A number of years ago one of our former baby-sitters asked for information on our ministry. That contact from the past became a contact for future support.

Friends

- Review your Christmas list.
- Review your parents' Christmas list.
- Review your wedding list, if married.
- Review your address book.
- Review your family's personal phone book.
- Remember people with whom you have shared hobbies, sports, and other interests.

My wife and I attended Murray State University in western Kentucky. At school, I led several Bible studies. One study met in the home of a dear couple. That couple was put on the guest list for our wedding and eventually added to our prospect support list. How exciting it has been to see them catch a vision for our ministry and begin to support us.

Contacts from Your Mission

Don't write off other missionaries too quickly. Often I have seen board members, missionaries, and mission staff take up support for a new missionary. That could also include administrators and personnel department staff. I think of one missionary couple who made an impression on one of our board members. The couple received not only financial support but gifts each Christmas and other expressions of love as well.

Friends from Other Missions

Logic might suggest that missionaries already have their own financial needs so don't support other missionaries. But missionaries are sold on missions. When it comes to giving, many missionaries enjoy sharing with those in other countries of the world. One veteran TEAM missionary faithfully supports one of our ICI couples.

Club and Civic Group Contacts

Don't forget contacts from such groups as Rotary, Kiwanis, Lions, Optimist, and so on; also, the PTO/PTA, neighborhood associations, Christian Businessmen's Association.

Miscellaneous

Do you have military contacts or belong to professional associations or unions? You might be able to contact corporations or foundations for support.

Caution: Attempting to enlist support from random corporations usually produces little. Therefore, be highly selective of foundations that you choose to approach. Identify someone with whom you have a relationship to be your advocate in approaching the decision makers.

As I added the name of a particular Christian foundation to my list, I admitted that I knew very little about it. But I watched for it to come up in conversation or to see the name in print.

One day I was speaking at a Bible college, and as I toured the campus beforehand, I noticed a plaque on a building. Reading the inscription, I discovered that the foundation on my list was responsible for the funding of that building.

I asked my guide about it, and he gave me the name of a key person who could introduce me to the foundation. I followed through on the contact, and our organization eventually received a gift from then.

As you develop your prospect list, pray for the people on it. Ask for the Lord to bring to mind the names of those you need to contact.

Do not write people off, assuming *he can't possibly help. He is already giving to six other Christian organizations,* or, *he can't help—he has three kids in college.*

Remember, you will never finish your list of prospects!

Several years ago an ICI missionary suggested that one of his donors might help our organization. The donor was a very successful Christian businessman. My first thought was that he was overcommitted and would not consider helping our mission. But fortunately, I didn't follow that initial inclination because it is my policy to follow up on *every* prospect. So I set up an appointment with him. Over the years, that man has continued to support our ministry.

By deciding not to place a person on your list, you make his decision for him. People need the opportunity to make their own choices.

Remember that God already has all the necessary people to provide your full support. You will expect some to support you who will not. But don't let that dishearten you. Wait on the Lord, and ask the Holy Spirit for wisdom to challenge potential donors.

After you have completed your list, invite a friend or relative to review it. Ask if he or she can think of other names to add.

Remember, you will never finish your list of prospects; you always need to be on the lookout for new ones. So let's move on to Step 3 where you will learn how to categorize your prospective supporters.

Self Guided Training

1. *Begin to compile your list of prospective donors. Check off each category after you have added the names from it to your list.*

Church friends
___ friends from home church
___ friends from current
church (if different)
___ friends from other churches
you have attended

Relatives
___ parents
___ brothers
___ sisters
___ grandparents
___ children
___ aunts/uncles
___ cousins
___ nieces/nephews
___ other

Neighbors
___ former
___ current

School contacts
___ grade school
___ junior high school
___ high school
___ junior college
___ college
___ graduate school

Employment
___ former part-time jobs
___ former full-time jobs
___ current job

Service contacts
___ barber/beautician
___ pediatrician
___ eye doctor
___ other doctor
___ accountant
___ home insurance agent

Service contacts continued
___ health insurance agent
___ car insurance agent
___ business insurance agent
___ lawyer
___ broker
___ banker
___ mechanic
___ plumber
___ nursery/preschool
teacher/baby-sitter
___ Avon lady
___ dry cleaners
___ dentist/orthodontist
___ family doctor
___ surgeon
___ specialists
___ printer
___ Christian bookstore owner
___ contractors
___ auto mechanic
___ others (review the Chamber of
Commerce directories)

Friends
___ your Christmas list
___ your parents' Christmas list
___ your wedding list (if married)
___ your address book
___ your family's personal
phone book
___ people with whom you've shared
hobbies, sports, and other interests

Contacts from your mission
___ missionaries
___ administrators
___ personnel department
___ board members

87

Self Guided Training

Friends from other missions
___ missionaries
___ administrators
___ personnel department
___ board members
Club and civic contacts
___ PTA/PTO
___ neighborhood associations
___ Christian Businessmen's Association
___ other (Rotary, Kiwanis, Lions, Optimist)
Miscellaneous
___ companies or foundations
___ other

2. *Geographically, where is your highest concentration of prospects?_____ Why?_____*
_____
_____

3. *Geographically, where is your second highest concentration of prospects?_____*
Why?_____
_____
_____

4. *Geographically, where is your third highest concentration of prospects? _____Why?_____*
_____
_____

Note: If a number of your prospects are in another area, check your calendar and mark the dates you have available to visit that area.

Group Guided Training

1. *Each person should begin to compile his prospect list and answer the questions above.*
2. *Brainstorm with your group about ways to think of prospective donors.*

Chapter 10

Andy was amazed by the number of friends he had listed. He had not thought of many of them for several years, but now good memories flashed across his mind, and a big smile crossed his face. He anticipated getting together with those friends and remembering good times with them.

But Andy was brought back to reality by the need to put the names into a systematic order. Was there a logical way to record and catalog the names?

Once you have gathered the names of potential donors from the sources recommended in Step 2, you will need to catalog them.

Cataloging Your List

The best way to catalog your names is to computerize them. However, if you do not have access to a personal computer, I recommend a four-by-six card system.

Prospect Card

Complete a card like the following for each of your prospects.

Step 3: Record and Catalog Prospects

12 Step System

Step 1	Begin with My Home Church
Step 2	Determine to Whom I Will Go for Support
Step 3	Record and Catalog Prospects
Step 4	Mail the First Prayer Letter
Step 5	Make Appointments
Step 6	Conduct the Visit
Step 7	Track Support
Step 8	Say Thank You
Step 9	Conduct a Letter/ Phone Strategy
Step 10	Expand Contacts
Step 11	Cultivate Support
Step 12	Resolicit for Support

```
                        (Front)
                                      $
                                      Amount Promised

Johnson, Daniel (Linda)      Dear
2736 Grove Avenue                    Form of Salutation
Chicago, IL 60647

Phone:  Home (312) 376-5127          Occupation:
        Office (312) 384-4200

Notes:  Uncle Joe's neighbor         Children: Bob-8 Sue-14
        Attends Whitewater Community Church

☐ Non-donor    ☐ Pledged gift donor    ☐ Special gift donor

            Potential Priority       ☐ High ☐ Med ☐ Low
            Estimated amount this
            person could give        $_____
```

When you begin, all of your cards will be filed under the category of "Non-Donors." However, as you proceed, you will need to file your cards alphabetically under: "Non-Donors," "Pledged Donors," and "Special Gift Donors" who do not pledge but choose to give periodically.

Donor Software

If you use a computer, there are numerous data bases that can be used. Both of these programs allow you to create your own form and gives you the ability to follow up on a future date and maintain an extensive diary on each donor. Here are a couple I would recommend:

1. Automated Contact Tracking (ACT).
Contact Software, International (214) 418-4885.

2. Maximizer –Maximizer Technologies, Inc.
1681 Chestnut Street, Suite 310, Vancouver,
BC Canada, V6J4M6, (800) 804-6299.

Prioritizing Contacts

Marking the "estimated amount each person could give" is a guess. But thinking through the following questions will help you make an educated guess and determine who might be "high priority" contacts.

1. What kind of home do they live in? (If it is rather significant, I would talk to them about giving a larger gift.)
2. Do they own more than one home, such as a summer home?
3. What kind of car do they drive?
4. Do they have extra sources of income? Royalties, income property, and so on?
5. What kind of lifestyle do they lead?
6. What kind of jobs do they have?
7. Are both husband and wife working full-time?
8. What is his job title or position?
9. Does the person own his own business? (Try to find out more about his or her business.)
10. Does he/she own more than one business?
11. How many people does he/she employ?
12. How is the business doing financially? (If possible, take a tour of the business.)

The previous questions will give you some idea of whether to ask for $30, $100, $150 or more. If a prospect owns his/her own business, you might talk about an annual gift of $1,000 to $5,000.

If you know a friend of a prospective donor, the friend may be able to help you determine a potential range of giving. You might say, "I am going to sit down with Mr. Smith and explain my support need. Do you think he would be capable of giving a gift in the range of $100 to $200? $3,000 to $5,000?"

The friend could then help you fine tune the figure you will project on the card.

If you talk to larger donors, you will rarely embarrass them by talking higher figures. In some cases, you compliment them by asking for a large amount.

It is better to aim high rather than low in the amount for which you ask. Why ask for $30 a month when the person could give $150?

On each card, you should rank prospects according to priority—high, medium, or low.

High-Priority Prospects

High-priority prospects are people who have good financial capability. Review the questions used to determine the range of a potential gift. That will help you decide which prospects can help significantly.

However, you may rank some donors as high priority based on their eagerness to support you. They have given you some signal to indicate that they want to be part of your support team, and now they are waiting to be asked.

Medium-Priority Prospects

Medium-priority are people who may not have great financial capability. They have not given you any particular signals that they will support you, yet it is likely that they will help. Therefore, you will pursue them after you have focused on your high-priority contacts.

Low-Priority Prospects

These are people with whom you have had casual contact. They are not strongly connected to you, but who knows? After you have pursued your high- and medium-priority people, these people may be potential donors.

Through the years I have found that identifying high, medium, and low priorities is essential. It is virtually impossible to give equal time to all the people who make up your prospect list. Therefore, you need to identify and spend time with those who will make the biggest impact on you and your ministry.

You will find some who will not qualify as either a high or medium priority in terms of financial capability but yet are committed to you in prayer. Be careful in your mind that you do not discount their value to your ministry. Their investment may even be more valuable than the financial ones.

Several years ago I met a young couple. I discovered that they had a love for the Lord's work and were good potential givers. They became high priority, and I devoted time to cultivating their friendship. Today I see in them a couple who not only began giving to our ministry but who has increased their giving. I'm grateful now that I established a system of priorities and that I took the time necessary to cultivate their friendship. Now let's build a basic giving schedule.

Potential	Number of Prospects
$150.00	II
$100.00	IIIII III
$ 75.00	IIIII IIII
$ 50.00	IIIII IIIII IIIII IIIII
$ 25.00	IIIII IIIII IIIII

Compile the following chart by reviewing each card and your estimate of that person or family's giving potential. Write down each specific amount, and indicate how many people fall into that category.

Identify your support goal. It should be determined between you and your mission at the time of your acceptance. My support goal is $_____ per month.

Use the information you have gathered to fill out a projected giving schedule that, when fully met, will provide your total goal.

Giving Schedule		
Potential	Number of Gifts Needed	Total
$150.00	2 people	$ 300
$100.00	8 people	$ 800
$ 75.00	9 people	$ 675
$ 50.00	20 people	$1,000
$ 25.00	15 people	$ 375 (2-A)
TOTAL	**54 people**	**$3,150**

Although your projection is an estimate, it serves to challenge your prospects to think bigger. Review your data; you need only fifty-four people to give in order for your plan to become a reality.

Another way to catalog your contacts is to do it geographically. You might identify, for example, a group of contacts in Los Angeles, a group in Grand Rapids, Michigan, and a group in Washington, D.C.

If possible, plan a trip to each of those key areas. Build each trip around high-priority prospects in that area. Then focus on medium-priority contacts, and fit in the low-priority contacts around the other appointments. Although your scheduling will not always fit the three categories, do what is possible to focus on your contacts by priority.

One final comment on geography. Maximize all of your contacts in a given area before moving on. For example, a new missionary candidate is graduating from Bible college. Before he returns home, he should make all his contacts for support in the area where he has lived and attended school during the last four years.

Does raising support still seem to be an insurmountable mountain?

Identify Your Top Ten Contacts

Does raising support still seem to be an insurmountable mountain? By systematically following the steps outlined in this book, you will find the climb easier. At this point, you've categorized a list of potential donors. Now you are ready to identify a top ten contact list. The purpose is to concentrate your efforts on a manageable number of people.

The Pareto principle states that 80 percent of the results flows out of 20 percent of the activity. To take advantage of this principle, you should focus on the top 20 percent by beginning with your list of the top ten potential donors.

Who should be placed on your top ten list of contacts? Separate the names of your high-priority contacts, and simply place them in order from one to ten. That makes your top ten list, which is where you will focus your energies with the hope of the best return on your investment of time and energy. You will want to pray for these "top ten" individuals in anticipation of calling each one for an appointment.

Initially, the top ten contacts will be from your non-donor prospects list. For the missionary who has already raised some support, the top ten list may include names taken from your pledged donor list, special donor list, or non-donor list. For example, after raising support for nine months, you may have a donor who has been supporting you from day one. Now he has been promoted in his job, and the Lord is blessing him financially. You sense that he could be recontacted to ask if he will upgrade his pledge. So you decide to include him on your top ten list.

As you prayerfully build your top ten list, ask the following questions.

1. Whom have I identified as being high priority? Pick your top ten from the names in the high-priority category.
2. Who has given signals that they are interested in my ministry? For example, who has said, "Let me know once you begin raising your support," or, "I would love to share in your ministry"?
3. Who has the financial capacity to make a big difference? That might be better determined as you find out what kind of job a prospective donor has. What position does he or she hold? Are both husband and wife working?
4. What is his lifestyle—home in which he lives, car he drives, and so on? That information will give you some indication of his financial capability.
5. Who can you visit most feasibly? For example, if you plan to be in Los Angeles for two weeks, who should you visit in that area? (In this case, in addition to visiting your high-priority contacts, you might contact medium- or low-priority donors simply because you are in the area.)
6. Who should I follow up with to help move closer to a decision to provide support?

Recognize that your top ten list will be constantly changing. When you have an appointment and a person on your top ten contact list pledges to your support, that name moves off the top ten list to your Donor Roster (see Step 7—Track Support). Now your list is down to nine, so you need to add another name.

Perhaps you meet a sharp prospective donor. That name will be added to your top ten list, and another name moves off. You may get word that one of your contacts is unable to give at this time. Move his or her name off your list, and add another name. Thus, your top ten list is in constant flux. In order to stay focused and maximize your energies, it is best to review it every week.

The following hints will be helpful in the early stages of working with a top ten list.

1. Initially choose people with whom you are comfortable. You need positive experiences to start you off.
2. Avoid appointments with mega gift donors until you have gained experience. I'm not recommending that you procrastinate for weeks or months, but gain some experience to put you in a positive mode. When you go to significant donors, go with confidence and boldness.

The following form will help you list your top ten contacts and force you to indicate what action you will take with each individual. You also need to indicate what amount you will challenge the prospect to give.

INNER CITY IMPACT
Weekly Support Raising Report

Mail to:

Name:_____

Address:_____

Inner City Impact
2704 W. North Avenue
Chicago, IL 60647

_____

_____

Phone #:(_____)_____

Due on every Monday:

1. A report on WHAT HAS BEEN ACHIEVED over the past week. (Retain a copy of each report for your records.)

2. GOALS for the new period of the 1st-15th.

3. Enclose most current copy of your Donor Roster.

This reporting period is:

___/____/____to____/____/____

CURRENT TOP 10 LEADS
(Donors or Non-Donors)

NAME	ACTION TO BE TAKEN					AMOUNT REQUESTED FREQUENCY (ie. $50./month) (ie. $150./quarterly)	RESULTS 1. Indicate what took place. 2. Indicate Future Action. Be specific and indicate date
	Phone for Appt.	One on One Appt.	Phone Appeal	Personal Letter Appeal	Group Meeting		

NOTE: The missionary need not necessarily take on all 10 leads within a given week.

INNER CITY IMPACT

MINIMAL SUPPORT I MUST RAISE MONTHLY	MY PERSONAL MONTHLY GOAL	ACTUAL PLEDGED MONTHLY TOTAL AS OF / / /
		*

*This amount must agree with your Donor Roster Report

Date last prayer letter was mailed: _____/_____/_____

Deputation Expenses

Please reimburse me from my account for deputation expenses totaling $_____.
(Receipts must be attached.)

Deputation Salary

Note: After 25% pledged monthly support has been secured, missionaries are permitted to draw out living expenses but an emergency fund ($300-single, $500-married) must not be used.

Please draw out $_____toward my deputation salary.

Date:___/_____/___ Signature:_____

Prayer Requests	Praises

How can we help?

Later, I will show you how to use this form to set goals and use the information for accountability.

1. *Use the card system to begin to develop your prospect list. Place a check mark by each category (see checklist in chapter 9) after you have listed all the names you can think of in a given category.*_____

_____

_____

2. *Determining estimated amounts and how you will prioritize a person may require additional homework and research. Begin this process.*_____

_____

_____

3. *Compile your top ten list.*_____

_____

_____

1. *Each individual in the group should complete the Self-Guided Training. Discuss the various categories.*

2. *Ask each person to discuss his top ten list and explain how he arrived at his decisions.*

Chapter 11

Andy can't wait to start support raising. But first things first. He needs to tell his friends about his new venture into missions, and the most practical way to do so is to send them a letter. Andy begins by writing down ideas he would like to communicate.

Because he has never written a letter like this before, he is somewhat apprehensive. Will people read it? Should he mention his need for money? Will people be offended? Is it too long?

Andy hopes that his letter will encourage people to start thinking and praying for him. After several drafts he is ready to mail it.

Now it's your turn. This chapter will give you a simple tool—a letter to inform potential donors that you are beginning to raise support. Note that this letter is not a substitute for the recommended one-on-one appointments. It merely sets the stage.

Writing the Initial Letter

Content

The letter should contain at least six components.

1. *The opening sentence should grab people's attention.* Many voices call for our attention, and we tend to simply glance through most mail. But people pay better attention to that which is well written. Thus, you want to catch and hold the reader with your first sentence. Consider these examples:
   > "What if your language had never been written before 1984?"
   > "What defines success? Many converts?
   > A New Testament finished?
   > Retiring after thirty years?"

2. *Introduce yourself to your reader and bring him up to date on your life.* Be brief in this section.

3. *Convey your burden.* People need to sense that you have been called of the Lord. Try to paint a picture of an individual you would like to impact through your ministry.

---

12 Step System

4. *State the name of your mission organization, and discuss its vision and outreach.* Ask your mission for a purpose statement that communicates its goals, and enclose a piece of literature about the mission with the letter.

5. *Inform the reader that you are 100 percent responsible for raising your own salary.* When explaining your financial goal, mention one-time expenses such as equipment needs and outgoing funds, if you are traveling overseas. Be specific; don't assume that your reader understands a missionary's financial needs. State your monthly goal: "I am responsible to raise $xxx per month."

6. *Provide the reader a means to respond to your financial need.* Enclose a business reply envelope from your mission. Be sure you know your mission's procedures for handling financial gifts.

Caution: When you talk about finances in a letter, it is easy for the recipient to agree to a lower figure than he could really give. You don't want someone who could commit $100 a month to pledge only $30. Although you will enclose an envelope, it is important that you don't rely on a response to that first letter. Use your letter to inform, and then ask for help when you meet with the potential donor one-on-one.

Helpful Hints

Keep the letter simple, and keep it short—one page, if possible. Avoid lengthy paragraphs. Edit and reedit. Misspelled words, poor grammar, and bad punctuation distract from the quality of your message. Rephrase sentences to remove unnecessary words. Ask a friend to read the letter and offer suggestions.

Type the letter neatly with sufficient white space and generous margins around your copy. Be creative. Use graphics. Your church office may have a clip art file from which you could glean suitable artwork.

A well-worded P.S. at the bottom of the letter is an effective way to grab attention. Add a personal handwritten note. Hand sign each letter.

Remember to include your address and the organization's name. Be sure the appropriate person from your mission approves your letter.

If possible print your letter using laser printer with personal salutations..

Contact your mission to see if you can take advantage of its bulk mail permit.

A sample prayer letter follows:

[Date]

Dear Friend,

¡Gracias a Dios por todo que El a hecho!—I thank the Lord for everything he has done. That is the language I will not only be hearing but speaking in the days to come as I prepare for missionary service in Spain.

After graduating from high school, I went on to study at Moody Bible Institute in Chicago. It was there that I developed a burden for missions. While I was at Moody I worked among Hispanics, and I have a real love and desire to minister with them in the future.

I will be serving with Missions for Spain, a Christian mission operating out of Madrid. They exist to see Hispanics saved and discipled and to see churches formed. I have enclosed a brochure on our mission.

The mission is requiring me to raise my entire support of $2,500 per month.

You are very important to me. You can count on my prayers, and in the weeks and months ahead I will keep you informed. I trust that God will use us both to make a difference in Spain.

Sincerely,

Becky Clark
Missions for Spain
1127 W. Adams
Chicago, IL 60606

Other Letters

During the deputation process the new missionary should send a prayer letter once a month to inform people about his progress toward the field. Keeping a diary of stories and happenings during the month will help you remember interesting information to put in the letter. The monthly prayer letters should be informational, not appeal letters.

Another way to place your need in front of people is to have your mission send a letter of introduction. A sample acceptance letter from Mission Aviation Fellowship (MAF) follows:[1]

[Date]

Dear Friend,

You'll be happy to know that Kevin and Linda Swanson have been accepted for service overseas with Mission Aviation Fellowship, with appointment to Latin America. We're happy, too, and warmly welcome them into our MAF missionary family.

I do not take lightly the responsibility that is mine to ensure that this gifted couple is placed in a position, not just to maximize their service for Christ but also to fulfill God's will in their lives.

The Lord has been preparing them through years of diligent training and varied experiences for this milestone. Valuable contributions from friends and relatives have influenced their lives as well. Above all, the redeeming grace and love of God have given motivation and daily enablement to pursue this goal.

Now that Kevin and Linda have completed all our application requirements, they will go forth to share God's call upon them with churches and friends. Let's pray together that they'll be well received, be given safety, and that those of God's choosing will join hands with them to provide the needed support to carry out their service to Christ. Perhaps you could open some doors of opportunity for them.

We want you to have the enclosed copy of their introductory folder—for yourself, or to pass on to someone else who may be interested. Additional brochures are available. Also included is a form that will answer

Mail the First Prayer Letter

questions that you or others may have regarding support policies and provisions. Should you desire any further information, please let us know.

In a few months we will send you an update on the progress of the Swansons. Thank you for your interest and concern for them and their ministry.

Very sincerely in Him,

M. H. Meyers
Chief Executive Officer

P.S. In case you are wondering—individuals and churches desiring to support the Swansons may begin support now, as anything not needed for immediate living expense will accrue toward their considerable travel and outgoing needs.

Following is an example of a letter from MAF that can be sent out by your mission midway through the support process:

[Date]
[Address]

Dear Mr. Friend,

We promised to keep you posted on the progress of Mike and Isobel and several months have now passed by. These have been busy and at times faith-testing days for them. But they have also been exciting days as they've watched God answer prayers! Thank you for the encouragement your prayers have brought.

Concerning their financial needs, they have reached the 65% mark in promised ministry support, but $1400 monthly is still lacking. Outgoing expenses are still needed. These include pre-field salary and related expenses $24,401; travel to Zaire $3800; shipping $5600; language school $3000 and passports, visas, customs, etc. $1000. Until their monthly support and outgoing expenses are met in full, the field budget will experience constraints that determine whether the opportunities before them can be fully met.

If God is challenging you to become involved with Mike and Isobel, now would be the perfect time to let them know by completing the form below and returning it to us as soon as possible. Let's pray that these financial needs may soon be cared for. Thank you for your interest in this dedicated family.

Sincerely in Christ,

(Mrs.) Phyllis Beiter
Ministry Partnership

( ) I will help send Mike and Isobel Dunkley to their assignment in Zaire by committing:

$_____per month $_____per quarter $_____per year in support of their ministry.

( ) I am enclosing a special gift of $_____for their outgoing expenses.

Resources

I encourage you to secure and read the books listed below. Each one devotes a chapter or more to writing effectively, and you'll gain much help in writing your prayer letters.

1. Rust, Brian, and Barry McLeish. *Support Raising Handbook—A Guide for Christian Workers.* Downers Grove, Ill.: InterVarsity, 1984.
2. Collins, Marjorie A. *A Manual for Today's Missionary.* Pasadena, Calif.: William Carey Library, 1986.
3. Collins, Marjorie A., *Who Cares About the Missionary?* Winona Lake, Ind.: Don Wardill, 1982.
4. Roberts, W. Dayton, and John A. Siewert. *Missions Handbook.* 14th ed. Monrovia, Calif.: Missions Advanced Research Comm., 1989.

5. Nichols, Sue. *Words on Target.* Richmond, Va.: John Knox, 1963.

6. Strunk, William, and E. B. White. *The Elements of Style.* 3d ed. New York: MacMillan, 1979.

7. Beach, Mark. *Editing Your Newsletter.* 3d ed. Portland, Oreg.: Coast to Coast, 1988.

8. McCasland, Dave. *How to Write Effective Newsletters.* Colorado Springs: The Navigators.

1. *Prepare the first draft of your initial letter, using the following components to measure your effectiveness. Grade yourself A, B, C, D on each component.*

Grade   **Component**

Content

_____   Did you grab the reader's attention?

_____   Did you briefly bring the person up to date with your life?

_____   Does your burden and vision show?

_____   Do you name and talk about the organization under which you will serve?

_____   Have you shared your financial need?

Layout

_____   Is the letter neatly typed?

_____   Do you have sufficient white space and generous margins?

_____   Are the paragraphs too lengthy?

_____   Did you use clip art or other graphics?

_____   Do you plan to add a personal handwritten note?

2. *Make necessary changes and rewrite your letter.*

3. *Find someone to proofread your letter.*

4. *Ask the appropriate person at your missions review and give final approval to your letter.*

5. *Print or duplicate your letter using a quality copy machine.*

6. *Remember to hand sign each letter.*

7. *Ask your mission organization if you can take advantage of its bulk mail permit.*

8. *Contact your mission organization to see if they will provide you with a letter of acceptance or introduction to be sent to prospective donors.*

Group Guided Training

1. *Each individual should write his or her letter and bring it to read to the group. Group members should offer constructive suggestions to improve letters.*

2. *Brainstorm on attention-getting opening sentences.*

3. *Group members may bring samples of missionary letters they have received and evaluate them for effectiveness according to the guidelines in this chapter.*

Note

1. Taken from MAF Ministry Partership Manual (used by permission).

Chapter 12

As Andy thought about the support raising principles he was learning, he remembered his maxim:

People give to people.
People give to people they know.
People give to people they know and trust.
People give to people they know and trust and care about.

Knowing that one-on-one visits provide the best way for people to get to know and trust him, Andy realized that he needed to start visiting his friends. His next step was to make appointments with them.

You are now ready for the challenge of making phone calls to set appointments with your friends. First, think about why this is important. What goals do you want to accomplish through the meeting?

- To become better acquainted.
- To share your excitement about ministry.
- To minister and enhance friendships.
- To provide the opportunity to give toward your support.
- To develop prayer partners.

The goal of each phone call is to make an appointment with a prospective donor.

Making the Phone Calls

Precede each call with prayer. If when you reach for the phone you find your heart pounding and hands sweating, welcome to the club. Many times I have closed my office door, taken a deep breath, prayed to the Lord, and grabbed the phone to make the call. Pray that you will speak the right words and be sensitive as you talk. Pray for an openness in those whom you call. Pray that God will work beyond your strategy to accomplish His will.

Plan to call first those people whom you believe will be most receptive. When I feel nervous, it helps me to call people whom I think will be receptive. Once I have successfully made those calls, the more difficult calls become easier.

Step 5:

Make Appointments

12 Step System

Sit at a quiet desk and work through a given section of your list in one evening. Once you've started, you should make twelve to fifteen calls per hour if you don't stop or delay. When you see the results at the end of the evening, you'll wonder why you were so hesitant.

In the case of a missionary couple, it is important that the wife call her own contacts. If she has a significant relationship with them and they know her better than her husband, they will respond more appropriately to her.

Assume that the prospective donors want to meet with you, and give them a choice. For example, say, "I really would like to meet with you. Would it be better this week or next week?" Or, "I would like to get together with you. Would you prefer Monday or Friday?"

Follow the old sales adage "Don't ask 'if,' ask 'which.' " "May I see you tomorrow?" leaves you more vulnerable than "What time can I see you tomorrow?"

Practice prior to your call. Adapt your phone script using words with which you are comfortable and which will best help you secure an appointment. When you have the script down pat, you will speak with more confidence.

As I talked with one of our ICI missionaries who was having difficulty securing appointments, I said, "Tell me what you say when you get on the phone."

He answered, "I say that I have just returned from college. Because I plan to be a missionary, I would like to meet with them."

I reminded him that wording makes a difference. I encouraged him to approach a potential donor on the phone saying, "I'm very excited about what God has in store for me, and I really want to meet with you. Would this week or next week be better?" Wording is important!

Helpful Hints

Be sure when somebody answers your call that you are talking to the right person. There is nothing more embarrassing than talking at length and then hearing, "Maybe you ought to talk to my dad." When calling couples, determine in advance whether you want to speak to the husband or the wife.

Be positive and sincere. Expect people to want to meet with you.

"Don't ask 'if,' ask 'which.' "

Show enthusiasm. Let people know you are excited. Smile as you talk.

Be brief and concise.

Avoid phoning at inconvenient times. For example, avoid calling families in the morning when Mom and Dad are getting the kids off to school. Avoid phoning at mealtimes. And it is usually unwise to call after 9:30 P.M.

However, when a potential donor is hard to reach, start calling at 9:30 P.M. Call every twenty minutes until you reach him. If he arrives home within those twenty minutes, he will not have time to get ready for bed and fall asleep before you call. Thus, you will not wake him.

Avoid asking for an appointment if you sense you are calling at an inconvenient time. Indicate that you realize it may not be a good time to talk, and ask when you can call back. When you return the call, create an environment in which you can get a positive response.

When you have had success in setting up an appointment, make another call immediately. You are likely to be more effective in your next phone call after successfully setting an appointment.

Do not discuss everything in a phone conversation that you intend to address in your meeting. The goal of your call is to assure the person that you have more to say.

Scheduling the Meeting

When Will You Meet?
Consider these times in which to set appointments during a one-week period.

Evening: Early evening (6:00 —7:00 P.M.)
Late evening (8:00 —9:30 P.M.)

Daytime: Breakfast
Lunch
Supper

Saturday and Sunday: Breakfast
Morning appointment
Lunch
Afternoon appointment
One or two evening appointments

Where Will You Meet?

Be flexible and willing to work around the other person's schedule. Offer to go where he is.

When one of our ICI staff called a prospective donor, the missionary received a typical response: the person said he could not meet because of his busy schedule. The ICI missionary asked if he could meet him on the construction site. That busy man who could not find twenty minutes for an appointment gave our missionary three hours of his time on the job site.

You cannot afford to be casual about your support. Therefore, think about places that you should not meet. Talking in the church hallway does not give you the time to talk seriously. Instead, set a definite place and time for an appointment.

If you are approaching a couple, try to meet with both of them. Think how discouraging it will be if you meet with the wife and she is excited about your ministry but then is unable to convince her husband to support you.

In rare cases, it may be better to meet with just one of the couple. For example, one might be very committed to giving whereas the other feels threatened. Or perhaps one spouse makes all the financial decisions.

If it is better to meet with one of the couple and that person is a professional, make sure all correspondence goes directly to the office.

How Long Will You Meet?

If possible, a one- to two-hour meeting is preferable, but 45-90 minutes might be more realistic. In such a setting you both can relax, take time to catch up with each other, go into detail on how God has led you, and discuss what you are doing.

With busy businesspeople who carve time out of jammed schedules, you may be fortunate to get twenty minutes. The key is to ask for a reasonable amount of time, and then be prepared to be flexible.

Agree with the other person on an appointment that gives you some flexibility in arrival. For example, ask for an appointment "between 10:00 and 10:15."

Calling Friends for the Appointment

It is advisable to rank your prospects according to those whom you need to call and visit first. The best way is to rank them: high-priority contacts, medium-priority contacts, and low-priority contacts as described in Step 3.

The better you know a person, the less formal and structured you need to be. That is the value of starting with your high-priority prospects. They often are easy to talk with and are more willing to make the appointment.

I was talking with one of our new ICI missionaries after she had raised her support, and I asked her, "By the way, how many people did you call for appointments who were unwilling to meet?"

She thought for a second and said, "Very few."

Phoning is easiest when you begin by calling people with whom you are comfortable.

Remember that the goal of your phone call is to make an appointment, *not* to ask for a decision on supporting you.

Begin by calling people with whom you are comfortable.

Step 1. *Identify yourself.* "This is Bill Dillon from Inner City Impact in Chicago. Is Bob Smith in?"

Step 2. *Be sure you have the right person.* Remember, in the case of couples, you need to decide in advance with whom you want to talk.

Step 3. *Engage in general conversation.* Talk about his family, career, church, mutual friends, hobbies, weather, or current events.
"Bob, it's good to talk with you again. How is your wife, Sue?
How are your two sons?"
"Is work going well?"
"Are you still active on the church board?"
Adapt your phone presentation, tone, and pace to put your phone partner at ease. When he is reserved, be reserved. When he is upbeat, be upbeat. This is called "vocal matching."[1]
Identify a similar experience that you share to develop rapport. What do you have in common? What will you say to someone who goes to your church? To a

111

mutual friend who lives in the same city? Think of some ice-breakers that you can use at any time.

Step 4. *State the reason for your call.* "I am planning to serve as a missionary and am anxious to meet with you and tell you more about the details of my ministry and the vision the Lord has given me."

Step 5. *Ask for the appointment.* "I really would like to meet with you. Would it be better this week or next week?"

Step 6. *Finalize details.* "That's great. I will plan to see you at 6:00 P.M. next Friday, September 17, at your home. Your home address is 2251 Pine—is that correct? Will you give me directions from the Kennedy Expressway?"

Step 7. *Wrap up your conversation.* "Sure looking forward to being with you. See you next Friday."

Calling Busy Businesspeople

In setting appointments with busy people, the key is to move the person to decide to meet with you. But that can be a long process. Be patient. Don't be discouraged when your prospect does not agree to see you within your time frame. Be persistent. Take good notes on when you should try again (and don't misplace the notes!).

Don't assume that a put-off means rejection. A busy person lives on a fast track, and you need to recognize that he may want to see you, but it will take time to fit you into his schedule.

Remember, the goal of your phone call is to set an appointment. If you don't set an appointment, the possibility is that you will not receive a support gift or the size gift you are praying to receive. Therefore, be resourceful in pursuing a busy person. Work hard to create alternatives. Constantly suggest other dates. Don't give up!

To avoid the appearance of being too pushy, however, do not leave your name with the secretary if the party is not available. Instead, state that you will try again, and ask when would be a better time to call. Thus, the person is not aware of your persistence.

Avoid calling busy people Monday morning when they are just beginning their week or late Friday afternoon when they are trying to wrap everything up before the weekend. That is a suggestion, though, not a concrete rule.

A call to a very busy businessman may go like this:

"Bill, I can't meet next week—I will be on business in New York. The following week I will be in Los Angeles. Next month I am preparing for our annual meeting. Then I am going on a golf outing down South, followed by a family vacation."

"I know you are extremely busy," you say. "It sounds as if we need to set a date for two months from now. Is there a date we can set now?"

"Well, to be honest, I don't like to set a date that far in advance because my schedule constantly changes."

You respond, "I understand that. When should I get back in touch with you to review your calendar? Can I give you a call in six weeks to set a date?"

The key is to end your conversation with a date set for you to call again. But don't be surprised when you call in six weeks and the man is out of town. You may have to try numerous times just to talk to him again. Then he may put you off for another two months.

The tendency could be for you to think that he is not interested and is trying to tell you that. Don't allow that negative thinking to discourage you. What he *is* communicating is that his life is hectic. Your persistence and pleasant follow-through can make the difference in the end.

After two years of follow-up calls with a certain person, I was able to get him to visit Inner City Impact. As he walked through our centers, met our staff, and viewed our video, I could see his excitement build. He turned to me and said, "I'm sorry I didn't set up this appointment months ago." Without any prompting on my part, he added, "This has been a very moving experience. I am going to send you a gift for your ministry."

Secretaries can be helpful in suggesting times to reach their bosses by phone. I tried to contact one man on numerous occasions. The secretary finally said, "He leaves by noon most days."

When I asked what time he got in to the office, she replied, "Seven A.M." So I called just after 7:00 A.M. and got through to him directly. In general, I have found that businesspeople are often accessible just before 9:00 A.M.

Listen to what people say about their schedules. One day I

had a phone conversation with a man who usually had his answering machine turned on at the office. When I reached him, he mentioned that he is always in his office on Fridays to meet with his men. Making a note on that, I made it my practice to call him on Fridays. And I always get through to him.

Avoid the tendency to give up on making a personal appointment and attempt to cover your needs by phone. Continue to pursue the one-on-one appointment because that is the way potential donors can look you in the eye, see your passion for the ministry, ask questions, and understand your vision more fully.

A number of years ago I called a very busy man to ask for an appointment. He said, "Why don't you just send me a letter and state your request?"

I said, "Sir, we really need to meet."

He said, reluctantly, "Well, OK. I can't give you a time now, but call me next week."

I called the next week, and again he asked if it was so important that we needed to get together. He repeated that I should put my request in writing. I reiterated that I thought it necessary that we meet. He reluctantly agreed and a date finally was set. I had gotten the appointment.

When we met, he loved our project. Eventually, he gave a substantial gift. Be persistent, and politely move people to a decision to meet with you.

Sample Script for Calling Referrals

Sometimes you will be calling people whom you do not know personally, who have been referred by other friends. When you call a referral, use the following format.

Step 1. *Begin by identifying yourself.* "This is Bill Dillon from Inner City Impact in Chicago. Is Don Jones in?"

Step 2. *Be sure you are speaking to the right person.* "Is this Don Jones?

Step 3. *Talk about the person who made the reference.* "A mutual friend of ours, Bob Davis, suggested that I contact you. I really have appreciated knowing Bob. He has been a big help to me, and he certainly speaks highly of you. He has a real heart for the Lord and missions." Or, "How long have you known Bob?"

Step 4. *Talk about the referral himself.* "Bob indicated that you are a dentist. How long have you been practicing?" "Bob mentioned that you are a member of First Baptist. How long have you been attending the church? I understand you teach a Sunday school class." If you feel comfortable, ask about his family, his work, and so on.

Step 5. *State the reason you are calling.* "Perhaps Bob mentioned to you that I am planning to serve as a missionary. I am anxious to meet with you and explain the details of my ministry and the vision the Lord has given me."

Step 6. *Ask for the appointment.* "I really would like to meet with you for about twenty to thirty minutes. Would it be better for you this week or next week?"

Step 7. *Finalize details.* "That's great. I will plan to see you at 6:00 P.M. next Friday, September 17, at your home. Your home address is 2251 Pine—is that correct? Will you give me directions from the Kennedy Expressway?"

Step 8. *Wrap up your conversation.* "I look forward to meeting with you. See you next Friday."

Caution: When calling a busy businessperson, you will probably not have time to engage in small talk because of his/her busy schedule. Move quickly to ask for the appointment.

Sample Confirmation Letter

If the appointment is set for more than a week in advance or if it is with a busy professional, it is wise to confirm the appointment by sending a letter similar to the following sample. Send the reminder letter the day you set the appointment.

Dear _____,

It was good talking with you on the phone today. I appreciate your willingness to learn more about ways in which God is working in my life.

We live in a time of unprecedented opportunity to share Christ. I know you are as excited as I am about the open doors for ministry God is giving me.

Thanks again for your interest. I'm looking forward to meeting you on [date and day of appointment] at [time of appointment] at [place of appointment].

Sincerely,

Note: To avoid confusion, I usually give both date and day.

Deal with an objection in two steps:

Part A: *Respond to the objection.*

Part B: *Ask for the appointment again.*

Handling Objections

As you seek appointments, some individuals will have objections. Handling those objections is the hardest part of support raising. Getting past them is essential.

Deal with an objection in two steps:

Part A: Respond to the objection.

Part B: Ask for the appointment again.

Objection: "I am already giving and can't handle any more missionaries. There really is no need for us to meet."

Objection: "We know the church is supporting you, so we don't see the need to get together."

Part A: Respond to the objection. "I can understand that, but I am anxious to update you on what the Lord has been doing. I can understand your concern but—"

Part B: Ask for the appointment again. "Would you at least give me that opportunity to meet with you? Would Monday next week be good, or would Wednesday be better?"

You must insist on meeting people one-on-one! Don't take a shortcut by asking for a financial commitment by phone.

Don't be discouraged by the over-committed donor. Your natural response is to agree that he is too committed to help. However, I would rather speak to an over-committed donor than to a non-donor who has never experienced the joy of giving.

Objection: "We heard your presentation at church Sunday evening, and we feel we already know quite a bit about your ministry."

Part A: Respond to the objection. "I am sure you do, but I am anxious to share more of what the Lord has been doing in my life and explain in detail what I will do in the ministry."

Part B: Ask for the appointment again. "Would Tuesday for breakfast be good, or do you prefer to meet over lunch?"

Objection: "I work downtown. I leave at 5:30 A.M. and don't get home until 7:30 P.M. every evening."

Part A: Respond to the objection. "I know you are extremely busy, but I would be more than happy to arrange my schedule downtown so we can have lunch together."

Part B: Ask for the appointment again. "How about lunch next Wednesday or Friday?"

Objection: "I am too busy to meet with you."

Part A: Respond to the objection. "I can understand that you are extremely busy. But I would be happy to have just fifteen minutes of your time so I can tell you about the burden and vision the Lord has given me."

Part B: Ask for the appointment again. "How about fifteen minutes next Wednesday or Friday?

Objection: "What is the purpose of our meeting?"

Objection: "Is this about finances?"

Objection: "Why do you want to meet with me?"

Part A: Respond to the objection. "I really want to tell you about the vision the Lord has given me and explain some of the details of the work to which the Lord has called me. I certainly will be prepared to share some of the opportunities for prayer and financial involvement."

Part B: Ask for the appointment again. "How does Tuesday or Thursday look on your schedule?"

Objection: "I am not interested in meeting with you, and I am sorry but I cannot be an encouragement to you."

Respond to the objection. "I can understand that. Thanks for taking the time to talk. I certainly could use your prayer support as I seek to respond to the challenge the Lord has given me. If it is all right with you, I will send my prayer letters to you so you will be aware of some of my prayer needs."

It is extremely important that you role-play your response to these objections. You need to be prepared to counteract any potential objections. MAF of Canada offers the following chart as you handle phone objections.

The following chart from Mission Aviation Fellowship (MAF) will provide you some guidelines in terms of number of calls you need to make in a week, people talked to, etc.

Handling Phone Objections

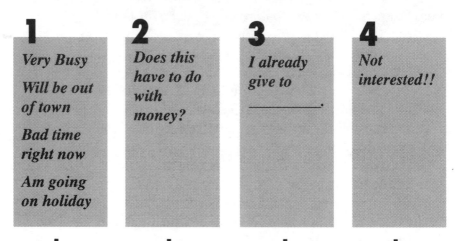

1

Very Busy

Will be out of town

Bad time right now

Am going on holiday

↓

I can understand that. These are busy times. Perhaps I can get back in touch with you when it is more convenient for you. How about _____?

2

Does this have to do with money?

↓

Well, part of it will be about money, but most of it will be informational. Of course, there is no obligation involved and I am sure you will be encouraged to hear about all the Lord is doing through Mission Aviation Fellowship.

3

I already give to _____.

↓

It is not my intention to detract you from your current involvement in any way. I would really like the opportunity to meet with you and tell you some of the things that are happening with Mission Aviation. I am sure you would be encouraged to hear about all that the Lord is doing.

4

Not interested!!

↓

I can appreciate your feelings _____.

You know, there is another way in which you can help me, if you would. I am asking people if they might be willing to pray for my ministry from time to time. Do you think that I could occasionally send you my personal prayer letters so that you can keep up to date on what is going on in the ministry?

WEEKLY SUPPORT TEAM DEVELOPMENT CHART

Name_____Sat. _____to Fri._____ Week # _____

YOUR GOAL	GUIDE-LINES	AREA	ACTUAL (CIRCLE AS YOU PROCESS)
_____	225	Calls made (i.e., number of times you dial the phone)	1 2 3 4 5 6 7 8 9 10 11 12 13 14 15 16 17 18 19 20 21 22 23 24 25 26 27 28 29 30 31 32 33 34 35 36 37 38 39 40 41 42 43 44 45 46 47 48 49 50 51 52 53 54 55 56 57 58 59 60 61 62 63 64 65 66 67 68 69 70 71 72 73 74 75 76 77 78 79 80 81 82 83 94 85 86 87 88 89 90 91 92 93 94 95 96 97 98 99 100 101 102 103 104 105 106 107 108 109 110 111 112 113 114 115 116 117 118 119 120 121 122 123 124 125 126 127 128 129 130 131 132 133 134 135 136 137 138 139 140 141 142 143 144 145 146 147 148 149 150 151 152 153 154 155 156 157 158 159 160 161 162 163 164 165 166 167 168 169 170 171 172 173 174 175 176 177 178 179 180 181 182 183 184 185 186 187 188 189 190 191 192 193 194 195 196 197 198 199 200 201 202 203 204 205 206 207 208 209 210 211 212 213 214 215 216 217 218 219 220 221 222 223 224 225
_____	45	People talked to	1 2 3 4 5 6 7 8 9 10 11 12 13 14 15 16 17 18 19 20 21 22 23 24 25 26 27 28 29 30 31 32 33 34 35 36 37 38 39 40 41 42 43 44 45 46 47 48 49 50
_____	22	Appointments set up	1 2 3 4 5 6 7 8 9 10 11 12 13 14 15 16 17 18 19 20 21 22 23 24 25 26 27 28 29 30
_____	0	Appointments kept	1 2 3 4 5 6 7 8 9 10 11 12 13 14 15 16 17 18 19 20 21 22 23 24 25 26 27 28 29 30
_____	0	Appointments not kept	1 2 3
_____	10	New ministry partners	1 2 3 4 5 6 7 8 9 10 11 12 13 14 15 16 17 18 19 20
_____	$200 weekly target	New monthly	5 10 15 20 25 30 35 40 45 50 55 60 65 70 75 80 85 90 95 100 105 110 115 120 125 130 135 140 145 150 155 160 165 170 175 180 185 190 195 200 205 210 220 230 240 245 250 255
_____	$400-500 weekly target	New special needs	50 100 150 200 250 300 350 400 450 500 550 600 650 700 750 800 850 900 950 1000

Troubleshooting Phone and Support Problems

MAF has provided the following analysis of causes and solutions of low areas in support raising.[2]

A "low area" is defined as "one that is significantly lower than the guidelines listed on the chart." For example, if you were to talk to thirty people about an appointment, about half, or fifteen people, should set up appointments with you. So if you talk to thirty people and only seven make appointments, then you should look under "Few appointments set" for a possible cause and solution.

Low Area	*Few calls made*

Possible cause	Laziness
Solution	Pray for enthusiasm about the opportunity to help others become a part of your ministry. Start moving and trusting God for the results.

Possible cause	Lack of contacts to call
Solution	If you ask each of your contacts for referrals, you will not have this problem. Stimulate a prospective donor's thinking by asking for names of the members of his Sunday school class. Ask if he has a church directory that he will go through with you. That may give you thirty to forty contacts.

Possible cause	Fear
Solution	Pray for courage. Remind yourself that you are doing potential donors a great favor to give them the opportunity to become a part of a people-changing ministry. Set definite times to sit at the phone and make calls.

Low Area	*Few people talked to*

Possible cause	Calling at bad times of the day
Solution	The best time to catch most business people is at home after supper (7:00 —9:30 P.M.).

Possible cause	Don't know how to get to husband
Solution	Ask his wife for the best time to catch him at home and for his office phone number. Check with the secretary to ask the best time to catch him at the office.

Low Area	*Few appointments set*

Possible cause	Not following prepared script
Solution	Start reading it!

Possible cause	Not speaking with enthusiasm
Solution	Ask God to make you enthusiastic. Practice reading the script with enthusiasm. After reading it fifty times it may seem canned to you, but it is fresh for each contact.

Low Area	*Appointments not being kept*

Possible cause	If a person does not show or forgets an appointment, you may not have sent a reminder or made the time clear.
Solution	Send a reminder letter, and clearly state appointment date, day, time, and place.

Possible cause	If you forget a meeting or are late, you may not be keeping an accurate appointment book, or you are not leaving your previous appointment soon enough.
Solution	Keep an accurate appointment book so that you do not forget any meetings. Map your route the night before, so you know where to go, how to get there, and when to leave one appointment to get to your next one.

Support Raising Statistics

Here are some statistics on raising support, compiled by Campus Crusade.[3]

But Steve Rentz of Campus Crusade reminds us that "As you make the calls remember it is up to God to motivate our donors. Above all we need to always maintain a Biblical perspective.

We must not see people as numbers but as individuals. Yes, we have to do the work but leave the results to God. And don't forget that God judges the motives of our heart.

If you dial your phone 225 times per month, you will talk to:

45 people and make

25 appointments that are kept by

20 people, and

10 of those people will support you with gifts of

$200 a month and $400-$500 for outgoing expenses.

If you raise $2,000 in monthly support in a four-month period, with an average gift of $25 a month, you need to raise $500 a month to reach your goal. On a weekly basis that is $125 a week. You would need eighty ministry partners—twenty new ministry partners every month, five weekly, and .7 every day.

For every three appointments you have, one will say yes to becoming a support partner.

If you have 240 completed appointments for support of $2,000 a month, you would need sixty appointments a month, fifteen a week, and 2.17 per day.

For every phone call you make, it will take three calls to make contact. For example, there will be times when you call and the party is not home. Or you might get a busy signal. Or they are not interested.

It will take 720 calls to set 240 appointments or 180 per month, 45 per week. These are completed calls, and you will need to talk to seven to eight people a day.

You have your work cut out for you. The important step is to set appointments with potential donors. Few people will call to set up an appointment with you; you are the one who needs to ask for their time. Block out two hours in the evening, and begin to call friends.

Self Guided Training

1. *Study and practice the phone script for Calling Friends for the Appointment using the steps described in the chapter. Practice making your call in front of a mirror. Choose a friend to play a specific prospective donor as you role-play setting up an appointment. (This can be more meaningful to you if you have in your mind a specific person you want to call.)*

2. *Study and practice the phone script for Calling Referrals using the eight steps given in the chapter. Practice making your call in front of a mirror. Choose a friend to role-play a conversation with you.*

3. *Review the objections in the text, and memorize a response to each one. Role-play handling the objections with a friend serving as the prospective donor. Give your partner the list of objections and the appropriate responses, and ask him/her to randomly choose the objections.*

4. *After several days of phoning, evaluate how successful you are in securing appointments. If you have not been very successful, review the material in this chapter. Especially review the section troubleshooting by MAF.*

Group Guided Training

1. *Pair off, and practice each of the suggestions in the Self-Guided Training.*

2. *Have partners role-play situations in front of the entire group.*

3. *Talk about problems that you foresee in phone conversations. Discuss ways to handle each obstacle.*

4. *Discuss your fears regarding making phone calls. Spend time praying together for God's guidance, timing, and provision of faith as you make appointments.*

5. *If possible and practical, have your missionary place a live call. Have each person report back on calls he made.*

Notes

1. Mission Aviation Fellowship of Canada. *Support Team Development Manual*, Guelph, ON: MAF, Canada, 1989.
2. MAF. *Ministry Partnership Manual*. Redlands, CA, p.271.
3. Statistics compiled by Steve Rentz, Campus Crusade.

Chapter 13

Today is a big day for Andy. He has an appointment to visit his former high school Sunday school teacher, Howard Kern, to ask him to be a part of his support team. This is the first time Andy will ask anyone for a financial gift.

Andy was up early this morning to spend his usual time with the Lord. Each promise he read from the Psalms seemed to apply to the 2:00 meeting with Mr. Kern. In fact, his prayer time, which he extended today, focused on that meeting.

Andy's emotions are mixed. He feels an excitement to see an old friend, yet he is nervous.

Preparing for the Visit

The time has come for you to venture forth from the comforts of your home or apartment into the "real world." It's time to actually meet with people—the heart and best part of support raising. It's time to become better acquainted with other members of the body of Christ and build relationships.

If you are scared or at least apprehensive, join the club. Making a personal visit can be an agitating aspect of support raising. Yet it also can be extremely satisfying.

Several years ago, I was asked to speak to the Board of Directors of a Christian ministry. As I stressed the importance of asking for a financial gift, a board member interrupted me to say, "Mr. Dillon, you don't understand. You see, I get nervous, my heart begins to race, my hands begin to sweat."

I interrupted her to say, "Ma'am, you have just described Bill Dillon. I get nervous, too, and it's natural to have those times when the heart begins to race."

Before we discuss how to conduct your visit, let's think about how you can prepare for it.

Appearance

Dress appropriately. Your clothes should be clean and neat and your hair well cared for. For a business call, men should wear a dress shirt and tie with a suit or sports coat. If the occasion is more casual, dress down but look presentable.

A book that I have found helpful is *Dress for Success,* by John T. Malloy. He also has written *Women's Dress for Success.*

Step 6:
Conduct the Visit

12 Step System

Step 1 Begin with My Home Church

Step 2 Determine to Whom I Will Go for Support

Step 3 Record and Catalog Prospects

Step 4 Mail the First Prayer Letter

Step 5 Make Appointments

Step 6 Conduct the Visit

Step 7 Track Support

Step 8 Say Thank You

Step 9 Conduct a Letter/ Phone Strategy

Step 10 Expand Contacts

Step 11 Cultivate Support

Step 12 Resolicit for Support

Breath/Body Odor

I always carry breath mints with me and recommend that you do the same. Deodorant, appropriate perfumes and colognes are a must.

Directions

Write down directions to your appointment the night before, along with a phone number to call in case you get lost. Allow sufficient travel time so that you arrive relaxed and confident. Racing into an appointment late or in the nick of time does not make a good impression.

Goal

The goal of your meeting is to ask the potential donor(s) to support you with his financial gifts and prayers. Therefore, it is important to be highly focused in your visit and move him to a point of decision.

Resist the temptation to ask the potential donor to do other things for you. For example, don't ask, Would you ask your pastor to set up an evening service for me? Could you call the missions chairman to set a time to meet with the missions committee? Could you invite twenty people to your home so I can share my ministry with them? You can find other opportunities to do that at a later date.

Time

Your appointments may be as brief as twenty minutes with a busy businessperson, or as long as two hours with a close friend. To accomplish your goal in twenty minutes, you must be brief and concise. That will require discipline and practice.

Review

Review whatever information you have about your prospect—his wife's name, family background, church attendance, work, hobbies, and interests. Review what each prospect may be able to give financially.

List Projects

In case he chooses to be a special gift donor, you should have a list of special needs to which he may give.

Project	Amount
Moving fund	$
Start-up fund	$
Car fund	$
Baby fund	$
Education fund	$

Pack

Bring whatever necessary literature, pledge cards, contribution reply envelope, video, and notebooks you will need.

Relax

Put yourself in a positive mood. Have you ever thought about how your mood and actions affect others? Recognize that future donors will respond to your mood. If you display friendly, sincere, and warm characteristics, a potential donor is likely to react the same way. Therefore, presenting yourself in a calm, competent, and relaxed manner is important. Relax, knowing that the person set the appointment because he is interested in what you are doing.

Pray

Pray! Pray! Pray! There is no better way to relax your mind and gather your courage than to pray before going into your appointment. Pray for courage, wisdom, and that all will go well. Do your best, and then leave the outcome in the Lord's hands. Remember He who calls you will provide for you. It's His work and His ministry.

Opening

Be prepared with opening phrases as you meet at the door. "It is so good to see you again. I have been looking forward to getting together."

Setting

As you walk into the office or home, take a quick look at the surroundings. A special picture, award, or object may suggest a special interest that the prospect has and a possible topic for conversation. For example, if the home is decorated with Western art, you might talk about that. If they have a special collection, ask basic questions such as, "How long have you been collecting?" "How did you get into collecting?"

When walking into the room in which you meet, allow your host to position himself first. Then position yourself so you can best converse with him. If you brought items to look at, you might suggest sitting around a table.

Six word pictures to guide your presentation.

Planning the Presentation

After you sit down, engage in brief informal conversation. Then cover each of the six sections listed below. To help you memorize these steps, I want to give you six word pictures.

You have been invited into the home of a prospective donor to make a presentation. You enter through the front door and are taken to the back of the house out to the backyard. Picture these six items in sequence.

1. In your left hand is a photo album.
2. In your right hand is a road map. In the backyard is a picnic table.
3. On the table is a globe.
4. On the table are a pair of reading glasses.
5. On the table is a blueprint.
6. In the backyard is a group of people dressed in uniforms with your name across them.

Let's review those pictures and discuss each item.

Album

The photo album in your left hand represents an update of your life. As you begin the meeting, bring the potential donor up to date with your life. Think of the photo album as organized by year. Go back to the time where you left off with the friendship, and tell him about your activities and goals from that time until now.

Map

The road map in your right hand represents how God has led you into ministry.

Globe

The globe on the picnic table represents world missions. Talk about your mission organization and how it fits into world evangelization.

Glasses

The reading glasses represent your vision. Talk about what you believe God is calling you do.

Blueprints

The blueprints represent your financial plan. Talk about your need for finances and your plan.

129

Uniforms

The people in uniforms with your name on them are on your support team. This is the point in your presentation when you ask the potential donor to join your team. Your goal is to bring him to a decision and ask him join the team.

The Actual Visit

The key is that you listen, listen, listen.

You should learn and practice the following outline so that it becomes second nature to you. Role-play an entire visit before you make your first one.

Section 1—*Bring the Person Up to Date with Your Life*

Some people you visit may not have seen you for months or even years. So start where you left off. For example, you have graduated from college, but the last time you talked extensively with this person may have been in your sophomore year of high school. Start with those high school years and review what has taken place in your life until today.

You also need to be brought up-to-date on your friend's life. Use the following questions to help.

"Since we met last what has happened in terms of your career?"

"Tell me about your family."

"Tell me about your children."

"How have you been involved in your church?"

"Have you developed any hobbies?"

"How do you use your free time?"

The key is that you listen, listen, listen. As you listen, you will learn more about the person, his family, interests, and personal needs. That will allow you to better pray for and minister to him.

When I called one prospective donor, he was excited to hear my voice. He asked how I was and how the ministry was doing. I talked about the ministry with him and asked him how his business and family were. It was then that he revealed that his wife had just asked for a divorce. I was ready to listen and to minister. I added him to my prayer list and mailed him a note assuring him of my prayers.

If you have prepared and role-played the visit in advance, you will be relaxed and able to listen. You will not be preoccupied with what you want to say. So do your homework, and practice, practice, practice.

Recognize that people will respond in different ways. You may encounter three different personality types.

The Expressive. Meeting with people and talking is enjoyable for this person. Because he enjoys talking, he will probably talk a great deal before you have an opportunity to jump in. Listen patiently, and be sincerely interested.

The Aggressive. This person will probably take charge and begin to ask questions about your ministry and involvement, often because he is curious. He will control the conversation.

When it is necessary to make a transition into section 2, the following phrase may be helpful: "Glad you asked. That brings me to my point—"

The Suppressive. He is quiet and leaves it to you to take charge and start the conversation. He will wait without giving you any indication of what is on his mind. But he is ready to listen to you.

Use these "cue" lines to keep your conversation moving.

"Could you tell me about—?"

"How did you do that—?"

"What did you do when—?"

"How did you feel about—?"

"You mean—, they did that—? Then what happened?"

Also use these listening recognition sounds to keep the conversation ball rolling.

"Uh-huh"

"I see."

"That's fascinating."

"Oh."[1]

Section 2—*Talk About How God Has Led You into Ministry*

When you need a transition sentence to steer the conversation to talk about how God has led you, you might say, "When we talked by phone to set up our time together, I indicated that I wanted to bring you up-to-date on what the Lord has been doing in my life."

Then do that. Start from the last time you saw the person, and talk about your *spiritual* journey since that point. It could mean you go back to your salvation testimony, your involvement with a local church, your burden, or how the Lord has allowed you to use your spiritual gifts.

Don't be lengthy, but show God's leading in specific ways. Give illustrations and tell stories of God's faithfulness. After you finish this section, there should be no doubt in the prospect's mind that God has led you and that you need to fulfill His purposes.

To ensure that you give a confident presentation, type a one- or two-page summary of the steps by which the Lord has led you to your present conviction that you are to serve in missions. It does not have to be in paragraph form but may be organized by numbered points.

You may refer to any or all of the following influences in your Christian experience:

• salvation decision
• influence of home church
• key Christians who have marked your life
• books you have read
• a crisis in your life
• exposure to missionaries
• key teachers and school subjects
• home influence

Place the influences in chronological order to help yourself rehearse the Lord's leading. Some call this an explanation of the "Lord's call to missions." Others who do not stress a special call to missions will explain the events as a growing conviction from the Lord that they should be missionaries.[2]

Section 3—*Talk About the Organization*

Now that you have brought the person up-to-date on your life and on God's leading, he needs to become acquainted with the organization with which you will work. Discuss any of the following points.

• The vision of your mission
• The fields in which the mission serves
• Distinctive of the mission (What makes it unique?)
• Where you will live
• Statistics of people to be served
• The leaders of the mission
• When you will leave for the field
• What is happening in your target field

Talk about your commitment to the organization. Show your excitement. Talk about how you are compatible with the mission's philosophy of ministry. Convey the assurance that you fully support the mission, its leadership, strategy, and policies.

If your organization has a quality videotape about the ministry, this would be a good place to show the video. Although a video cannot be shown during short, twenty-minute presentations, it can add a great deal to a longer appointment. When making the appointment, verify that the home or office has a VCR available.

Also show the person any literature you have about the organization. If you do this, however, it is important that you hold the literature for your prospect. Do not hand it to him, or he will start reading it and you will have lost his attention. If the person takes it, say, "Let me take you through it." Then reach out and take the pamphlet back.

Section 4—*Share Your Vision*

It is vital that people catch your vision. People don't give to a need; they give to a vision!

You need to convey your burden with *conviction.*

You need to convey your burden with *emotion.*

You need to convey your burden with *sincerity.*

You need to convey your burden with *confidence.*

To help articulate your vision, write out your response to the following:

1. *Identify specific reasons that you joined this mission organization.* _____

_____

2. *Describe the specific ministry to which you are assigned.*

_____

_____

3. *Explain why your personal ministry is important.*

_____

_____

4. *Describe what you want to achieve through your ministry. Set goals that are realistic and measurable.*[3] _____

_____

_____

You might begin this way: "I firmly believe God has called me to serve with the ABC Mission. My job will be to

_____. *My vision is* _____."

Several years ago, Sharon Murphy, one of our new missionaries at ICI, put her vision this way: "My vision is to see these inner city girls saved, to see them discipled, to see them attend a Christian college, marry a Christian young man, and establish a Christian home." Now I see her vision realized. She graduated from the Moody Bible Institute, and two of the young girls she discipled also attended Moody.

If your vision is for children and the Lord has allowed you to work with children, then focus on one young person with whom you have worked in the past. Paint a picture for your friends of how you affected that little one's life. Here is an example.

I will never forget the first day Juan came to our ministry. He was a tough Puerto Rican boy no older than nine years of age. One night he didn't like the way things were going with the ministry. He grabbed some of his friends, walked down the three flights of stairs, picked up a rock, and put it right through my car window. I began to invest time with that tough boy, and he came to know the Lord. Now he is going to church with me and planning to go to Bible school.

Potential supporters want to be introduced to real people. Statistics alone will not impress them. So paint a picture to help them catch your burden for the lost. Put God's fingerprints all over the ministry. Whatever your dazzling vision may be, be enthusiastic and convey it to others.

After sharing your vision, seek a response by asking one of the following questions.

"Does this give you a better idea of what we will be doing?"

"Does this generate any questions on your part?"

"Do you see the value of what we will be doing?"

"Any comments?"

Write down your vision, take time to practice presenting it, tell it to a friend, and get it down pat. As you meet with Baby Boomers, you will learn that they want specifics. If they are to donate $1,000 a year to your ministry, they want to know what the $1,000 will do. Tell them why you are going and what results you will see. Talk about giving them a return on their investment. Be specific. Talk about ministry impact!

Section 5—*Share Your Financial Need*

It is significant that God has led you, has caused you to be identified with a Christian organization, and has given you a vision. Now your potential donor must be made aware of what you need.

To stop before sharing your need conveys the message that you don't need his help. However, your needs as a missionary are significant, and the body of Christ must be made aware of those needs so they can intelligently and prayerfully consider their role in meeting them.

Introduce your need using these words: "The Christian organization that I have been called by God to serve with has given me the responsibility of raising one hundred percent of my personal support. It is my job to seek friends who are committed to me and to my vision to help meet my support need."

At this point, ask your friend if he or she understands how the support system works. Some people have no idea that you must ask individuals to pledge toward your support. Ask, "Are you familiar with how missionaries on support must raise their funds?" If he is not, give a more thorough explanation.

Next discuss the components that make up that support (a factor that varies from mission to mission). Also, explain what that means in terms of dollars, without going into unnecessary detail.

"The mission organization has asked me to raise the following:

Salary	$xxx
Insurance	$xxx
Administrative cost	$xxx
Retirements	$xxx
Projects	$xxx
Travel	$xxx
Start-up costs	$xxx
	$xxx

The total need per month is $xxx."

Now, pause and ask if he has any questions. That will give you an opportunity to hear what is going through his mind and answer questions and handle objections. If you don't deal with those now, your prospective donor may sidestep your question when you ask for support later.

Most missionary organizations will take a certain percentage from each missionary's income to help cover some of the mission's overhead—costs to maintain the mission headquarters, secretaries, receptionists, training, and so on. That is the "administrative cost." Some donors will suggest that they do not understand or want to give money toward administrative costs. The way you respond is critical. Enthusiastically support your mission and its policy, and be prepared to defend that policy. Without your mission's expertise, office assistance, and resources, you would be on your own. Although administrative costs don't cover your actual expenses, the organization's costs help keep you on the field.

Also, it would be wise here to explain your commitment to the individual donor. Campus Crusade identifies at least three commitments:

1. To serve faithfully.
2. To communicate regularly what God is doing through your ministry.
3. To share prayer concerns with one another.

Section 6—*Ask for Specific Help*

If you have done your job, it ought to be clear to your friend that God is active in your life. You are a part of an exciting ministry, and you and the organization are faced with significant opportunities. There is one last question to be discussed—what can he or she do to help meet your need?

You may give the best presentation of your life and answer all your prospect's questions. But if you fail to ask him directly to become one of your donors, is it not likely that he will volunteer his financial support.

If you have done your homework before the appointment, you will have already estimated the range you would like to ask your friend to give.

Explain your strategy for raising the support. "To reach my goal of $_____, I am looking for individuals who will be able to pledge personally toward my support. I am looking for people who could support me at $___ or $___ per month."

Let's say I am asking the person to give $50 per month. I would quote two amounts that are higher. You want to help people raise their level of giving, and increase their vision.

"To reach my goal of $___, I am looking for individuals who will join my team and be able to pledge personally toward my support. I am looking for people, for example, who could support me at $100 or $75 per month."

The next question is the most critical question of the entire visit. So before you ask it,
* slow down your pace,
* pause,
* make sure you have eye contact,
* put a smile on your face,
* speak with sincerity, and
* speak with confidence and boldness.

Ask him to support you. "I really want you to be a part of my support team. I need your help. Would you support me at $50 per month?"

Campus Crusade prefers to ask people to support them at $1, $2, $3, $4 a day which is like asking for $30, $60, $90 or $120 per month. You may want to frame the figure in a daily rate.

Also, you may want to ask in terms of a range, if you choose not to state a specific amount. For example, "I am looking for people who could support me in the range of $50 to $100 per month or more."

Wording is everything. You need to use words that you are comfortable with. Avoid words that will be vague or weak, such as: "I am sure you probably have other places you are giving but maybe you would think of helping me." Or, "Would you give this some thought?" You need your potential donor to make a decision, not just think about it!

After you have asked the question, be quiet. Let the person think about it. You will want to break the silence and look for excuses for him/her, but be completely silent.

I will never forget a good friend of our ministry who was excited about our vision. I sat down with him, shared the vision, and proceeded to ask him for a very sizable gift. Then I remained quiet and saw drops of sweat rolling down his face. I kept quiet until he said, "OK, I will do it."

Bring the Person to a Point of Decision

Once the silence is broken, he will come back with one of four responses.

Response 1: *"Yes, I would be glad to support you at $xxx."* Ask if he is prepared to make a check out right now. That will minimize your follow-up effort.

If he cannot give the check to you immediately, encourage

Ask him to support you.

him to start the support as soon as possible, and suggest a date. "Would it be possible for you to send your first gift by _____?"

Be sure to clarify the amount of the gift and the frequency. Also, it is wise to explain the process by which your mission handles gifts.

Response 2: *"No, we are unable to support you at that level at this time."* You can respond in several ways.

Your Response - Part 1: "Would you feel comfortable with $40 [instead of $50]?"

That may prove to be effective if they are looking for a way to support you, but the suggested amount was too high. Or ask, "What would you feel comfortable giving?"

If they say no to that, ask one other question.

Your Response - Part 2: Ask for a special gift. The conversation could go like this: "Not only do I have to raise my monthly pledged support, but there are special needs that I have such as _____. You indicate that you feel you cannot make a pledge at this time—would it be possible for you to make a special gift?"

You can ask for a specific amount or give a range. "Would it be possible to make a special gift of $150?" Or, "Could you make a special gift in the range of $100 to $150?"

If for some reason that seems inappropriate, you might word it this way: "You indicate that you feel you cannot make a pledge at this time. Would it be possible to make a special gift between now and [the end of the year or by a certain date]?" Notice I used the words *special gift*. I do not like to say *one-time gift*. The term *one-time gift* gives the impression that it is the last gift this donor will ever give.

Some givers do not want to be committed to a pledge but like to respond as needs arise. They are spontaneous givers. I call them *special gift donors,* and they play a big role in your support strategy. A missionary always has special projects that need funding. Talk about one specific need with this donor, and ask for a special gift. For example, it would be natural for a foreign missionary to explain outgoing expenses. You should have several projects or needs in mind from which he or she could choose, and it is your responsibility to find which is of greatest interest to him.

You will be amazed at the number of special gifts that can be captured in this way. Also, recognize that if you do your job of thanking and loving those people through time, some will continue to give future special gifts, and some of them will eventually become pledged donors. But it all begins with that initial visit when you ask for a gift.

Inner City Impact has numerous special gift donors. Every quarter I call one specific donor and give him an update. He asks for a letter and, like clockwork, several hundred dollars come back in the mail. I have learned his style and rhythm in giving.

Some individuals will give you the impression that they want to help, but it is impossible. To that kind of person, you might say, "I sense that you really want to help but find it difficult at this time. Is that right?"

Then plan to make future contact with that person because circumstances do change.

A second kind of person who says no simply is not interested. Recognize that, and graciously thank him for his time, but indicate that you would appreciate his prayer support.

Response 3: *"We need some time to review our commitments and pray about this matter. I don't believe we can give you an answer tonight."* Answer by saying, "Can I answer any additional questions for you? Is there any further information you need from me?"

After they respond to that question, the next words out of your mouth are critical. Remember, you want to move people to a point of decision. In this case, you need to prepare for a follow-up call. If worded properly, you will have an open door to walk through when you make that call. Give the individual forty-eight hours, and use the following wording: "Can I get back to you on Thursday? Will that give you enough time to make a decision?"

Then try to agree on a range of time when you may call. "How about if I call between seven and nine Thursday evening?"

If they need more time beyond the forty-eight-hour follow-up call recommended, you might send a reminder letter. You want this letter to arrive a day before the follow-up date. Below is a sample letter.

> Dear _____,
>
> It was good to visit with you and share my vision for ministry. Thanks for taking time to meet with me.
>
> You will recall that we agreed that I would call Thursday evening sometime between 7:00 and 9:00 P.M. I look forward to talking to you then about your decision. Have a great day.
>
> Sincerely,

You are moving again toward a decision, and you have

identified that the next step will be a phone call. If the potential donor says that he or she will call you, say, "It would be better for me to contact you." It is always better to have control of the next move.

On my follow-up call I say, "Hi, this is Bill Dillon. You will recall that we agreed I would get back in touch with you today regarding my support. Have you had a chance to come to a decision?"

The individual will respond in one of three ways: yes, no, or he has not made a decision.

If the answer is, "Yes, I do want to support you," thank him enthusiastically; clarify the amount and the frequency of his gift and then make plans to pick up the check. When you pick up the check, ask him for referrals.

If it is impossible or impractical to pick up the check personally, ask him to agree on a date by which he will send it. If he does not have a contribution envelope, mail one to him.

If the check does not come in on or near the date as promised, call him again. "Last time we talked, you indicated that you would be mailing your first gift by _____. For some reason, we have not received your gift, and I am wondering if it might have been lost in the mail."

If you make your first follow-up call and he has not yet made a decision, try to identify his potential concerns and seek to answer them. Then ask, "When can I get back to you? What about next Thursday? Will that give you enough time to make a decision?" Keep pursuing him as long as is practical until he decides.

If he says no when you call, respond as described below.

Response 4: *We cannot provide either a pledge or a special gift.* You do not want to be pushy. He has done exactly what you wanted him to do—come to a point of decision. Thus you need to read him very carefully to determine which of two reactions you are getting.

1. From his body language or words you get the signal, "I really like you. I believe in what you are doing, and I wish I could help you but, I'm sorry, I simply can't help at this time."

If that is the case say, "When would be a good time in the future to get back in touch with you? When might your circumstances change?" You may add, "I do want to remain in touch with you. Would you permit me to send my prayer letter so you can pray for me?"

2. From his body language or words, you get the signal, "You are not a high priority to me. I am not interested in your cause. You are wasting your time and mine."

When you get that signal, graciously thank him for his time and do not pursue him by mail or otherwise. When someone says no, I initially feel discouraged and let down. But soon I remember that it is not a personal attack against me. The Lord will provide for my needs.

Be prepared for people to say no. It is a fact that not everyone will support you. You will be turned down from time to time, and you will not enjoy this part of support raising. But if you continue to work through your network of people, those who say no will not be the norm.

Handling Objections

Besides those four responses, you can anticipate other objections. Here is a brief list of some of those objections and ideas for how to respond to each.

Objection: "We give to our church and do not help other individuals."

Response: "It is very important that you give to your local church and that they can count on your support. But if our vision is to be realized, we need the help of individuals like you. The reason our organization exists is because no specific church or denomination is meeting this particular need."

Objection: "Doesn't our church support you?"

Response: "Yes, they do, but our total need is $xxx per month, and the church is only able to support us at $xxx per month. We deeply appreciate the commitment of the church, and we are excited to represent it. But we must find individuals who can lend their support as well."

Objection: "We are already supporting other missionaries."

Response: Explain what is distinctive about your organization or mission, for example, "We are the only Christian organization reaching the XYZ tribe in South America. How else will they hear the gospel?"

Objection: "We have just had a financial setback."

Response: "I am sorry to hear that. I certainly will remember you in prayer, and I will pray that the Lord will make it possible for you to participate at a later date. When should I plan to get back in conduct with you?"

Objection: "I can't say I have ever heard of your organization."

Response: Try to identify Christian leaders or pastors they know who speak highly of your organization. Also identify any associations or organizations with which your mission is associated that they might know.

Objection: "My income fluctuates and I am not sure I can make a pledge." (The person may work on commissions or receive bonuses that are hard to predict.)

Response: "I understand that. Is there a particular time of the year when you receive your income? Do you receive it quarterly, for example?"

Once you know the pattern, maintain contact with him through your monthly prayer letter and perhaps a phone call or personal letter once a quarter. When calling, I use these words: "I want to keep in touch with you and give you updates on my ministry."

Approximately fifteen days before his income arrives, call and give him an update on your ministry. Indicate that you will call shortly after he receives his bonus. The purpose of that call will be to discuss how he can become involved.

The goal is to keep your ministry in front of him. It will be easy for him to forget you, so you need to take the initiative.

One man I know decides how much he will give each year once he knows the size of his bonus check. I know when that bonus check comes, but throughout the year I call and keep ICI in front of him. Every year Inner City Impact receives a good-sized check from him.

Objection: "Well, what is the minimum pledge you are looking for?"

Response: "I would love to be able to count on a gift of $_____." Don't give a minimum. Tell the person what you would like him or her to give. It is important to get people to raise their sights beyond the minimum.

What other objections do you anticipate? How will you

respond to them? Take a minute to jot them down.

MAF, Canada and Eric Floreen, provide eight important principles to remember when dealing with possible objections.[4]

1. Listen to the concern.

2. Respond to the concern. "I really appreciate the fact that you want to think it over and make a decision based on what the Lord wants you to do."

3. Clarify. "Just to help me clarify my understanding, what questions do you need to work out in your mind?"

4. Allow the potential donor to answer, listen carefully, and ask relevant questions. "In addition to that concern, are there any other reasons you would hesitate to join the team?"

5. Thank the person for clarifying his concerns. "I appreciate your openness. I am not here to pressure you into making a bad decision, but I would like to be able to give you enough information to make a good one."

6. Answer his concerns. "Does that fully answer your questions?"

7. Reexplain the need. "As I mentioned earlier, we are excited about what God is doing through our ministry. I am looking for the Lord to raise up a team. I sincerely believe that through an investment in my ministry, you can have a vital part in touching the lives of people."

8. Ask again. "I would love to have you on my team. Because of the urgent nature of my work, I would like to know as quickly as possible who will be involved in my ministry. Do you think I can count on you to be part of my prayer and financial support team?"

In sum, there are three points to remember in dealing with the uncommitted.

1. Clarify the concern.

2. Answer the concern.

3. Ask in principle.

Some organizations have a commitment form to be signed by the donor as he makes his commitment to you. It could be as simple as:

___$1 a day ($30 per month)

___$2 a day ($60 per month)

___$3 a day ($90 per month)

___$4 a day ($120 per month)

___$ (other)

Also, there is a place for the person to provide his address:

Name _____

Address _____

City _____ State_____ Zip_____

Phone (home) _____ Work _____

Signature _____ Date _____

You may also include the following options:

___Check enclosed

___Dates check will be picked up

___Date check will be sent

A form like this could be made in triplicate with one copy for the donor, one copy for your records, and one copy for the mission. Betty Barnett in her book *Friend Raising* suggests leaving the following sheet with your new supporters.

> *This sheet may save you some confusion as you send in your support for my ministry.*
>
> 1. Please make out your checks to [agency name] so that you will receive a tax-deductible receipt. Because of U.S. government regulations for non-profit organizations like ours, you should not have my name written anywhere on the check. You can enclose a slip designating it for my support, or indicate that on the remittance envelope flap.
> 2. Please feel free to enclose personal letters along with your check in the envelope. I would love to hear from you!
> 3. Because my records are kept up to date, you can send a check to cover several months at a time to make things more convenient for you, and to entail less paperwork.
> 4. If at all possible, please send in monthly support during the first half of the month. This helps me with my monthly bills, and it may be easier for you to remember, too.
> 5. Thank you again for your generosity and your partnership with me in this missionary work. *I do appreciate you!*

Closing the Visit

If your visit is with a busy businessperson, it is important that you guard your time carefully. Stay within the time agreed upon. If you need more time, ask for permission to extend your meeting or consider rescheduling it.

If your prospect is not pressured for time, consider spending additional time in fellowship. The more time you spend with him, the more you will help make him feel a special part of your support team.

As you conclude your presentation, you may be tempted to talk about other ways he can help you. But if you are highly focused, you will take one thing at a time. The purpose of this visit is to seek financial and prayer support. If this person becomes part of your team, you can go back later, and ask him to participate in other ways. (There is an exception to this rule. If you do not have the occasion to see this person on a regular basis you might have to discuss other business such as referrals.)

When you are ready to close your visit, that is an ideal time to get his commitment to pray for you. If you have designed a prayer card, leave that and ask for his daily prayer support. And ask if he has prayer requests for which you can pray.

Thank him for his time and leave some literature. Then close by praying for him, his family, career, and the ministry the Lord has given you.

After the Visit

Immediately after the visit take a pad of paper, a cassette recorder, or a laptop computer and record your notes on the visit. If your spouse is with you, one of you can record these things as the other drives home. If you are alone, you might drive several blocks, pull the car to the side of the road, and recall everything you can about your conversation. If you wait too long, you will forget vital details.

Here is a sample of the things you could note. The more you know the better.

Spouse's name
Children's names and ages
Birthdays
Anniversary
Hobbies
Prayer requests
Hometown
Career(s)
If owner of his own company—product, profit, competition
Names of other ministries they support

Giving patterns, i.e., when they give
  (monthly, quarterly, end of the year)
How much they give
How they give—through their church? Stock?
Projects they like to support
Projects they do not like to support
Names of future prospects
Churches they have attended
Names of mutual friends
Name of missions chairman at the church
Ways you can thank them
  (they like to read—give them a Christian book)
Organizations to which they belong
Directions to home or office
Secretary's name

Within the next twenty-four hours, follow up with a letter thanking him for seeing you and reciting any commitment that he made. People will appreciate your promptness.

Role-Play the Visit

One important part of training is to role-play the visit, using the above principles. Each mission should offer a training program that will teach the missionary how to be successful in the visit. But if you do not have such training available, ask a friend to role-play a visit with you. Ask him to critique your presentation.

Begin by picturing in your mind a person with whom you would like to have an appointment. Answer these questions as you set the stage in your mind.

Name?
Age?
Career?
When did you last see him?
What amount will you ask for?

Remember, practice makes perfect. The more you perfect your presentation by presenting it to people, the more relaxed you will become.

Keep the following time guidelines in mind for each of the six sections of your twenty-, thirty-, or forty-five-minute presentation. Of course, these are suggested times; each situation will vary.

	20 min.	30 min.	45 min.
Section 1—Bring the person up to date with your life	4	6	15
Section 2—Talk about how God has led you into ministry	3	4	5
Section 3—Talk about the organization	4*	8*	10*
Section 4—Share your vision	3	4	5
Section 5—Share your financial need	3	4	5
Section 6—Ask for his specific help	3	4	5

*This does not take into consideration time you might need to show a videotape on your ministry.

If you find that few people are investing or you are receiving a low pledge amount, MAF suggests the following:[5]

Low area	*Few people investing*
Possible cause	Not a clear presentation
Solution	Pray for clarity, and practice your presentation.
Possible cause	Unenthusiastic presentation
Solution	Pray for enthusiasm during your presentation.
Possible cause	Not asking for investments
Solution	Follow the script and wait silently for the reply.
Low area	*Low pledge amount—few pledges and more special gifts*
Possible cause	Not stating a definite amount, so people are giving $15 or less per month, or a lump sum
Solution	Say, "I'm looking for people to invest $25 or $30 or $35 per month."
Possible cause	Unclear in communicating that you are looking for monthly investments
Solution	Clearly ask for monthly investments.

After each visit it is important that you track your support, which you will learn to do in the next chapter.

147

Self Guided Training

1. *Memorize the six word pictures and what they represent to help you remember the six sections of your presentation.*

2. *Write out your personalized script using these six sections as an outline._____*

_____

_____

_____

_____

_____

_____

3. *Practice role-playing until the six steps of the visit seem natural to you. Picture in your mind a person with whom you would like to have an appointment. Have your friend evaluate each of the six sections of your presentation by writing what was done well and which areas need improvement.*

Also role-play how you will handle the four responses that you might encounter. Role-play with a friend other objections that you might receive.

4. *In preparation for your actual visits, obtain from your mission organization the following:*

• A quality video tape of the ministry (if available). If it is appropriate to incorporate into your presentation, obtain a personal copy of that video.

• Appropriate literature. Make sure you read it from cover to cover.

• An adequate supply of business reply envelopes for gifts.

1. *Bring these six items to show with the word pictures: photo album, road map, globe, reading glasses, blueprint, and a uniform. Teach the six word pictures in the following steps.*

> **Step 1.** *The teacher recites aloud the six word pictures without any explanation of what they represent.*

> **Step 2.** *The class recites aloud the six word pictures without any explanation of what they represent.*

> **Step 3.** *A member of the class volunteers to recite aloud the six word pictures without any explanation of what they represent.*

> **Step 4.** *The teacher recites aloud the six word pictures with an explanation of what each represents.*

> **Step 5.** *The class recites aloud the six word pictures with an explanation of what each represents.*

> **Step 6.** *A member of the class volunteers to recite aloud the six word pictures with an explanation of what each represents.*

> **Step 7.** *Divide group into twos. Each partner should tell the other the six word pictures with an explanation of what they represent.*

2. *Each person should write out his personalized script using the six sections as an outline. (See Self-Guided Training question 2.)*

3. *The instructor should choose a volunteer to act as the potential donor to role-play with the instructor the entire presentation in front of the group.*

Note: In each role-play, have the person picture in his mind an individual with whom he would like to have an appointment. Answer these questions to set the stage: Name? Age? Career? When did you last see him? For what amount will you ask him?

Group
Guided

Training

Group
Guided

Training

4. *Divide group members into twos. Each person will go through his entire presentation with his partner.*

5. *Ask volunteers to give their presentation to the group. The group will critique each presentation by evaluating each of the six sections. Be sure that any negative comments are followed by suggestions for improvements. Encourage positive comments.*

6. *A volunteer acts as the potential donor and role-plays with the instructor how he will handle the four responses that he may encounter.*

7. *Divide group members into twos. Each person will go through how he would handle the four responses that he might encounter.*

8. *Ask volunteers to go before the entire group, and role-play how they would handle the four responses that they might encounter.*

Note: If you have access to a video camera and VCR, I would recommend that you video tape the actual presentation of each missionary, and then critique it.

Notes

1. Mission Aviation Fellowship of Canada. *Support Team Development Manual*. Guelph, ON: MAF, Canada, 1989.
2. "Big Picture" Dennis Carlson, Send International. Notes.
3. Mission Aviation Fellowship of Canada. *Support Team Development Manual*.
4. Ibid.
5. Mission Aviation Fellowship of Canada. *Ministry Partnership Manual*. Redland, CA p. 271.

Chapter 14

Andy left Mr. Kern's house feeling very positive. He had enjoyed reviewing memories of his high school days and was surprised and pleased to know that Mr. Kern was still interested in him. In fact, Mr. Kern promised both to support Andy financially and to pray for him daily. Support raising by visiting friends was turning out to be a positive experience.

The next day Andy wondered, *Did Mr. Kern promise $50 or $60 a month support? I think it was $50—but maybe it was $60.*

Another question plagued Andy. Did Mr. Kern promise to begin his support June 1 or July 1? Because they had talked about July 4 in their conversation, Andy thought they'd agreed on a beginning date of July 1. But he wasn't sure.

It was clear to Andy that he couldn't rely on his memory. He needed to develop a system of recording vital information after making a visit.

You need a system to tell you what support has been pledged, what has been paid, what is expected to come in, and with whom you need to follow up. As a new missionary, you began with a list of contacts. Although they were non-donors, you thought of them as prospects. It is your job to move these people to a point of deciding to support you financially and in prayer.

The Donor Roster

A donor roster will enable you to track your prospects. They eventually will fall into three categories: pledged donor, special gift donor, and undecided.

As you determine where each prospective donor falls, place his name on a list under the appropriate category. The categorization helps you see exactly where you are in terms of current support.

Step 7:

Track Support

12 Step System

Step 1	Begin with My Home Church	
Step 2	Determine to Whom I Will Go for Support	
Step 3	Record and Catalog Prospects	
Step 4	Mail the First Prayer Letter	
Step 5	Make Appointments	
Step 6	Conduct the Visit	
Step 7	Track Support	
Step 8	Say Thank You	
Step 9	Conduct a Letter/ Phone Strategy	
Step 10	Expand Contacts	
Step 11	Cultivate Support	
Step 12	Resolicit for Support	

DONOR ROSTER

Today's Date: ___/___/___

Missionary Name _____

Pledged Donors

Name	Amt. Pledged	Frequency	Date of Pledge	Jan	Feb	Mar	Apr	May	Jun	Jul	Aug	Sep	Oct	Nov	Dec
Jim Jones	$50	Mo.	01/01/91	15	50		50								
Bob Evans	$150	Quarter	03/15/91				150								

Actual Giving by Month

Total Pledged Monthly:

Total Received Monthly:

* Note: Convert Quarterly and Annual Pledges into Monthly
* Note: It is your responsibility to determine beyond the shadow of a doubt if a gift is a Pledge or a Special Gift

Special Gift Donors

Name

Date of 1st Gift

Actual Giving by Month

	Jan	Feb	Mar	Apr	May	Jun	Jul	Aug	Sep	Oct	Nov	Dec

Total Received by Monthly:

Undecided

Name

Date Asked

Follow-up Date

Follow-up Date

Follow-up Date

Follow-up Date

Follow-up Date

Follow-up Date

Pledged Donors

Note the heading called "Pledged Donors." Reading from left to right, you find a place for the donor's name, followed by the amount he has agreed to pledge and the frequency. The three most likely frequencies of giving are monthly, quarterly, and annually. That is important because when you know how frequently each donor contributes, you know how much money to expect.

As people promise support, you add the date when each person decides to support you. To the right is where you keep actual records of each donor's giving by month.

Don't forget that as a donor makes his pledge, you should ask if he can start that pledge immediately. So if he makes a pledge on July 4, you should expect to see his first pledge paid during July. If July passes and you receive no gift, and August comes and goes, the Donor Roster alerts you to a problem. You need to get on the phone and find out what happened.

Near the bottom of the front page you can calculate your totals. There are two totals: total pledged and a monthly total of actual giving.

As you review the actual giving of each donor, you will notice five trends.

1. A donor is giving exactly what he promised.
2. A donor increased his pledge.
3. A donor stopped giving.
4. A donor gave a special gift.
5. A donor decreased his giving.

Every action on a donor's part requires an action in response from you. When someone increases his support, thank him. The donor, excited because he is giving more, will be waiting for your response of gratitude. How many missionaries fail to acknowledge that increase?

If someone has stopped giving, call that person and find out why.

If someone gave a special gift, discover the reason, if possible. Maybe it was an annual bonus. If so, make a note to ask for a special gift next year, fifteen days before he receives his bonus.

If someone decreased his giving, find out the reason. Maybe it was due to financial problems—a layoff, perhaps. That person needs your prayers and understanding.

When you receive a surprise, first-time gift, contact the giver, thank him, and determine if he intends to be a pledged donor or a special gift donor.

Every action on a donor's part requires an action in response from you.

Special Gift Donors

On the second page of the Donor Roster is space for special gifts and undecided donors. In the section for special gift donors, you will not find "amount pledged" or "frequency" columns because they have not made that commitment. Total the special gifts that come in each month.

There is a place to enter the date of the first special gift, and to track gifts if that person continues to give. By watching his giving by month, you will note whether he has a pattern. Never forget that the special gift donor could become a pledged donor if you do a good job of thanking him, loving him, and keeping him informed.

In reviewing the Special Gift Donor section, note the need to which a donor responded, and ask him to give toward a similar project in the future. For example, you requested funds for an emergency in January and again in July. He responded to both. He is likely to respond to future emergencies.

Undecided

The final section is undecided. Remember your goal is to move everyone to a point of decision. So keep the names of undecided persons in front of you, and follow up on them. If you don't, the undecided will get lost in the shuffle. As you follow up, some undecideds will make the decision to take on your support.

Tracking the undecided is not optional. When an individual requests time to make a decision, try to get him to agree to a follow-up within forty-eight hours.

In this section, note the date you first asked a contact for a gift. Then enter future follow-up dates.

This form will be invaluable to you for tracking purposes. And it has another use. I recommend that you become accountable to someone within your mission. Each time you mail a report, photocopy the master sheet, add the date, and mail it to the person to whom you are accountable. It is a good way to assure him or her that you are making contacts and progress.

Support Raising Report

A second tracking form is a support raising report (see chapter 10, page 96). New missionaries should make such a report weekly, and the mission should monitor them weekly. Once a person has raised full support, the accountability may be cut back to every two weeks or once a month.

This report is tied to the concept discussed in Step 3 of working with your top ten contacts.

For it to be successful, use the same support raising form for two different reports. The first covers the goals you set for the previous week and a record of what action you took to achieve them. The second report includes goals you set for the next week.

Begin the Support Raising Report by entering the date of the current week. Then enter your top ten contacts.

For each contact you need to decide what action you will take. You have five options: (1) phone for an appointment, (2) conduct a one-on-one visit, (3) appeal for support by phone (see Step 9), (4) appeal for support by personal letter (see Step 9), (5) conduct a group meeting, i.e., church meeting.

The next part of this form—amount requested and frequency—also requires decision making on your part. If you already decided the amount for which you would ask when making your card file, enter that amount. If not, decide on an amount now, and enter it on this form.

The last section deals with results. You are asked to provide: (1) what took place and (2) what future action you will take (be specific and indicate date). You will not complete this portion until the action has been completed and you are ready to turn the report in to the person holding you accountable for that week.

Keeping these two simple forms up to date will help you immensely as you track your support.

1. *Name the three kinds of people that the Donor Roster form will track.* _____

_____

2. *What are the three probable frequencies of giving that you will encounter?* _____

_____

3. *What five trends should you be alert to as you review your donors' giving on the Donor Roster?* _____

_____

Self Guided Training

4. *Because every action of a pledged donor requires a reaction on your part, identify what action you need to take for each of the five trends listed above.*_____

_____

5. *Enter your top ten contacts on your weekly report. Complete the entire form. List not only the names but the action you expect to take and the amount with which you plan to challenge them as well as the frequency of giving.*

6. *Identify a person in your mission to whom you can be accountable. Plan to submit the weekly report each week and an updated Donor Roster.*_____

_____

7. *As you complete action on your top ten list, add the results to your Donor Roster.*

8. *If you are a missionary already on the field, go through your records and post the last six to twelve months of your donors' giving on the Donor Roster.*

9. *Next look for the five trends and take the appropriate action. As needed, contact your donors.* _____

_____

_____

_____

Group Guided Training

1. *Each person should complete the Self-Guided Training. As a group, discuss ways that these forms will help you in deputation.*

2. *Work on the following case studies to determine what action you will take after interpreting the five trends in each case study. You can handle these case studies in several ways.*

a. *Have each individual prepare his response as a homework assignment.*

b. *Break into small groups and discuss the case studies.*

c. *Discuss the case studies with the entire group.*

Case Study 1

Andy was reviewing his Donor Roster and noticed that one of his donors, Sandy Taylor, had been giving $50 a month for the last year. But the last three months her gift had been $35. What might be some reasons for her decreased giving? What would you advise Andy to do? Explain.

Case Study 2

Andy has appreciated the support Dave and Barb Gemar have given in monthly checks of $100 in the last year. But last month, in addition to their $100 monthly gift, there was another check for $75. What should Andy do? Explain.

Case Study 3

Andy has been blessed to have his former college roommate Clive Craigen and his wife, Randi, giving $75 each month. For some reason, however, they have not given a gift in the last two months. What might be some reasons for them to stop giving? What would you advise Andy to do? Explain.

Case Study 4

Andy was excited when he reviewed Sherry Hervey's giving. For the last eighteen months, she supported Andy at a level of $60 a month. Last month she increased her giving to $75. What should Andy do? Explain.

Chapter 15

Andy had just checked with his mission and was encouraged to learn that gifts were coming in for his support. Mr. Kern's first gift had come in, and Andy's former roommate, Dave Woodier, and his wife, Jayna, sent a special gift of $100. In addition, his home church had begun its support.

As he thought about his friends, Andy realized that he had never thanked them for their gifts. They had opened their homes to him, listened intently to his vision, opened their hearts and checkbooks. And he had failed to thank them personally.

Andy immediately took out stationery and began to write. "Dear Mr. Kern, thank you so much for your gift of—"

Why do some missionaries have a difficult time establishing consistent givers?

Why do some donors never give a second gift?

Why do some donors drop support?

Many answers can be found to these questions, but I am convinced that many donors stop giving because the missionary fails to say thank you. Thus, you need to decide that expressing appreciation will be a part of your ministry.

The apostle Paul had a thankful heart and often expressed his appreciation to fellow believers.

> *"I thank my God through Jesus Christ for all of you, because your faith is being reported all over the world." (Rom. 1:8)*

> *"I always thank God for you because of his grace given you in Christ Jesus." (1 Cor. 1:4)*

> *"I thank my God every time I remember you." (Phil. 1:3)*

Paul's heart of thankfulness led to another action on his part—prayer for fellow believers.

> *"We always thank God, the Father of our Lord Jesus Christ, when we pray for you." (Col. 1:3)*

> *"We always thank God for all of you, mentioning you in our prayers." (1 Thess. 1:2)*

Step 8:
Say Thank You

12 Step System

Step 1	Begin with My Home Church
Step 2	Determine to Whom I Will Go for Support
Step 3	Record and Catalog Prospects
Step 4	Mail the First Prayer Letter
Step 5	Make Appointments
Step 6	Conduct the Visit
Step 7	Track Support
Step 8	Say Thank You
Step 9	Conduct a Letter/ Phone Strategy
Step 10	Expand Contacts
Step 11	Cultivate Support
Step 12	Resolicit for Support

It is important to develop a thankful heart and express your thankfulness both to the Lord in prayer for those who support you, and to the donors themselves. Saying thank you will make the difference between a one-time gift and an excited donor who grows in his interest and commitment to you. My dad taught me that lesson, and people still remember how quick my dad was to recognize and appreciate people's generosity.

I remember meeting with one individual who decided to support several of our missionaries. When the missionaries failed to say thank you, he asked me, "Didn't they get my gift? Didn't they need it? Didn't they appreciate it?" Hurt by the lack of appreciation, he did not want to be hurt again. He chose not to send future gifts to those missionaries who had not learned the importance of the words thank you. However, I continue to say thank you to that donor, and he continues to send thousands of dollars to our organization.

Three principles about saying thank you have revolutionized my life. They are not complex, but the key is to apply them day in and day out.

1. Say thank you.
2. Say thank you immediately.
3. Say thank you immediately in writing.

Say Thank You to the New Donor

If you handle the first gift from a new donor properly and the person feels appreciated, he is likely to send a second gift. You may have a valued friend who will increase his or her giving and introduce you to other potential donors. Consider these scenarios.

A person has responded to your request, and you know him.

The size of the gift may dictate your action. If the person sent a sizable gift, you should call immediately and thank him and follow up with a personal letter. If the gift was modest, you may respond with a personal letter. The key is to say thank you, immediately, and in writing.

When you write or call, clarify with your first-time donor whether the gift is to be considered a pledge or a special gift.

A person gives a gift, and you have no idea who he is or how he knows about your ministry.

The size of the gift again dictates your action. If the gift is sizable, you should call immediately and thank him. Try to set an appointment to meet and become acquainted. Learn more about him, his family, church, and career.

Also, immediately send a personal letter of thanks for the gift and express how pleased you were to talk by phone. Then thank the Lord for His answer to your prayer that He work beyond your strategies.

If you were recommended to the new donor by another person, call or write the referrer to thank him. In the future, ask him if he knows other people you can contact. Always seek to build an expanding network of people to be part of your support team.

If the gift was a modest gift, you may respond with a personal letter. Thank him and encourage him in his ongoing support. You might suggest that $xxx be pledged per month, and ask if he would be part of your monthly support team. You need to know if he will contribute monthly, quarterly, annually, or if his was a special gift.

Therein lies the value of tracking your donors. Obviously each new person should be added to your mailing list. If, after a period of time, he does not respond with a monthly pledge, look for an opportunity to ask him for a special gift.

What to Include in a Thank You Letter

Every gift must be acknowledged—ideally within twenty-four hours, but more realistically within one week. And each thank you letter should include the following:

Acknowledge the amount.
Say thank you.
State some results of your ministry.
Keep it brief.
Be neat.
Be prompt.

This sample thank you letter meets those six criteria.

> August 7, 1999
>
> Dear Bernie and Kathy:
>
> Just a note to let you know how much I appreciate your recent gift of $45 for our ministry here at ICI.
> These last few weeks have been packed with excitement. Day camp ended with three kids being saved the last day, and just last week we arrived back from summer camp. We really watched the Lord work.
> Again, thanks, Bernie and Kathy, and do say hello to your sons, Jamison and Corey, as well.

To save time compose a master thank-you letter each month. As you acknowledge each gift, personalize the master letter. For example, I want to send a thank you to my former Sunday school teacher Fred Zoellin and his wife, Joan.

Paragraph 1 Same paragraph as in model monthly letter and add "It's so nice to have my favorite Sunday school teacher praying for and giving to my work."

Paragraph 2 Same paragraph as in model monthly letter.

Paragraph 3 Personalize this paragraph.

Be sure to change the master letter each month.

Some missionaries use pre-printed letters in which they fill in the blank based on the gift. That may save time, but it is not as personal or effective as a personal letter.

When to Say Thank You

Remember to say thank you each time:

- you receive a special gift of any size.
- a pledged donor sends a special gift above and beyond his or her pledged support.
- a special donor begins to support you monthly.
- a pledged donor or special donor upgrades his or her financial gift.

By maintaining the Donor Roster (see chapter 14), you will note when a gift comes in and can respond immediately. If you fail to respond, you indicate that you are not sensitive to your donors.

Send a letter when:

- a person has entertained you either in his home or by taking you out to eat.
- a person has performed special services for you, such as assisting you in doing your taxes, calling a pastor to set up a meeting for you, or inviting a friend to see a presentation of your ministry.
- someone sent a special birthday, anniversary, or baby gift.
- a person has provided special favors such as overnight housing, meeting arrangements, gifts of clothing, or food.

In essence, any time someone does something special for you, you should recognize that generosity and say thank you.

God has given you a special role as a missionary, and many of the Lord's servants are waiting to minister to you. You'll be excited to see the resources the Lord will bring to you. But remember, givers need to be thanked and appreciated.

One time as I sat in the dentist chair, I talked with the dentist about my missionary work. As I left, he said simply, "There will be no charge. God bless you in your work."

I went home and remembered my three principles: Say thank you, immediately, and in writing. So I sent him a thank you letter.

Several months later, my wife and three children went to the same dentist. Again, there was no charge. And after their visit, I said thank you, immediately, and in writing.

Several months later, one of our inner city young people had a dental emergency. I called the dentist and he kept his office open long enough to see us and, again, charged us nothing.

God multiplied the dentist's initial ministry to me, and I'm convinced that my saying two simple words—thank you—made the difference.

How to Say Thank You

The most important way to say thank you is to say it verbally and in writing. But let me add that there are many other creative ways to express your appreciation. You can do one or several of the following:

Send flowers. What kind do they like? What color do they like? Try to make that extra effort to find out.

Send candy. What kind does he like? Chocolate? What kind of chocolate? What brand? The more you know about the individual, the better you can thank him.

Send a book.

Give a gift certificate. Is there a particular store in which that person enjoys shopping? A Christian bookstore?

Observe what people like. Remember to listen, listen, listen. Is she a chocolate lover? Do they have a particular collection? Is he into a particular sport?

Wycliffe uses the letters T-A-P in its training to identify three areas in which you can thank people.

1. Being appreciated for Things can be "a warm fuzzy," i.e., "I like your dress."
2. Being appreciated for Accomplishments is more meaningful, i.e., "You did well on the test."
3. Being appreciated for Personality traits is most meaningful, i.e., "You really are a considerate person. Thank you for seeing that I needed to sit down."

Wycliffe also recommends that you follow three steps in composing a letter:

1. Mention the Things, Accomplishments, or Personality (TAP) for which you want to compliment him or her.
2. Say thank you.
3. Mention in one line how you feel about them.

Dear Howard and Lois:

Thank you for taking us to meet the missions committee. You certainly have done a lot to lead that group from sending one missionary to sending twelve this year! You really know how to run a meeting. No wonder you get so much done. Thanks much!

Dear Joe and Joan,

You have always been the most encouraging people to be around! Your enthusiasm for the Lord and commitment is an inspiration to both Sue and me. Thank you for listening. Thank you for caring. Your lives model Christ.

Dear Bob and Jessie,

Thank you for having us in your lovely home. The bed was so comfortable and your home so lovely. We really enjoyed it.

Phrases of Appreciation

Often missionaries look for special ways or words to express appreciation. Following is a list compiled by Wycliffe to help you say thank you.[1] Note the focus on the use of the word *you*. Focus on the donor and make him feel a part of the team.

You are a continual source of joy and encouragement to us as you faithfully pray and stand with us financially.

I wonder if you realize that you have been a partner with us for eight years now.

Each time your check comes we realize that your prayers back it up. That is such an encouragement.

The Lord overwhelms us with joy through your faithfulness to us.

As Paul said to his partners, your funds are a fragrant offering, a sacrifice acceptable and pleasing to God.

Your prayers and financial investment cause us to praise God for His goodness.

Each month when our statement of funds comes and we find your name listed there, we stop and thank the Lord for you.

Whenever the Lord uses us in some special way, we're reminded that you are also a part of it.

Your prayers make a difference in our lives and work. And, of course, your faithfulness in funding this ministry is so helpful and encouraging. I hope you know what a joy you are to us.

Without you and others standing with us, it wouldn't be possible to serve Him in the task of helping fulfill the Great Commission.

Isn't it good to know that God is producing lasting fruit through our partnership?

In heaven you'll meet many dear people who have come to Christ partly because of our ministry together in helping get the Word to them.

You, through your prayers and finances, are the Lord's way of sowing His Word that brings living souls to Himself forever. And now you are involved in sowing the seed among the Uspantecos. All praise to the Lord.

Wonderful friends like you are a blessing from the Lord. When you are so good to us, my heart's reaction is to start looking for someone to whom I can be an answer to prayer also. Thank you and thank the Lord!

If anyone needs to convey thanks it is the Christian worker, and we can learn from others who have expressed their thanks as above. Remember, appreciation isn't appreciation until it's expressed. Express it!

Salutations

Vary your opening salutation in letters: "Hi!" "Greetings from Ghana!" "Hi there—Whoosh! That was time passing." "Dear Special Friend," "Dear Ones," "Dear Partners in Prayer."

Closings

Use various closings in your monthly letters: "In His love," "Partners with you," "In His fellowship," "Gratefully His in the Service of the King," "In His Name," "In Christ's service," "Jesus loves you and so do we," "Joyfully serving Him," "Have a happy day," "Your partners in missions," "Your brother in Him."

Three Donor Rights

In our world today we often think in terms of rights. Let's apply that to your donor—the donor has three rights.

1. He has the right to know whether you received the money or gift.
2. He has the right to know whether you needed the money or gift.
3. He has the right to know whether the gift was appreciated.

A simple thank you says that you care and fulfills the basic rights of your donor. May the Lord give you a good ministry as you thank people.

1. *Identify three people who have done something for you recently. Write to each one, and tell him how much you appreciate him.*_____

2. *What are the three key principles in saying thank you?*

_____

_____

3. *When should you say thank you? (Fill in the blanks.)*
After you receive a _____ *gift.*
After a pledged donor sends a special gift _____

_____   _____

After a special donor begins supporting you on a
_____*basis.*
After a pledged donor or special donor has _____
_____*his or her financial gift.*

4. *In our world today we often think in terms of rights. What are the three donor's rights given in this chapter?*_____

_____

_____

5. *Write a master thank you letter that you can use next month. Commit to a time when you will finish it.*_____

_____

Individuals should complete the Self-Guided Training. Discuss ways you want people to thank you. Then brainstorm with other group members about additional ways you can say thank you to various kinds of donors.

Note

1. Wycliffe Partnership Development.

Chapter 16

Andy's days and especially his evenings were filled with support-raising activities. After visiting contacts in the evening, he sent thank you letters and updated his Donor Roster the next morning.

In reviewing his list of potential donors, Andy noted that his friends were scattered across the country. Keith and Debbie Rundquist, college friends, lived in New Jersey. Liz Stern, a former neighbor, lived in California. And Freddie Vasquez was now married to Andrea and lived in Calgary.

Andy reflected on his individual friends, and memories began to surface. He wished he could visit each one in person, but time and money would not permit that. Yet he wanted them on his support team. How should he communicate his need?

In earlier chapters you read that the best support-raising stratcgy is to visit people one-on-one. Though you should visit as many prospects as possible, sometimes a long-distance trip is out of the question. What should you do then?

Now is the time to use a combination of letters and telephone calls to reach those people whom you cannot visit. Letter and phone contacts will be made as you are making personal visits. Because it requires less time and effort, you may be tempted to fall back on this strategy for those who live nearby. But don't get lazy! You need to meet one-on-one with as many people as possible.

The following outlines are adapted from Campus Crusade.[1]

Outline for a Support-Raising
Letter to Someone You Know

A. Acknowledge the person reading the letter. Ask an open-ended question to draw him/her into the letter.

B. Say something personal about yourself (a brief glimpse at your life).

C. Say something about how God led you to join the mission, your ministry assignment, and how your work will have an impact (your personal vision).

D. Indicate appreciation for the reader and his/her interest in you.

Step 9:
Conduct a Letter/Phone Strategy

12 Step System

Step 1 Begin with My Home Church

Step 2 Determine to Whom I Will Go for Support

Step 3 Record and Catalog Prospects

Step 4 Mail the First Prayer Letter

Step 5 Make Appointments

Step 6 Conduct the Visit

Step 7 Track Support

Step 8 Say Thank You

Step 9 Conduct a Letter/Phone Strategy

Step 10 Expand Contacts

Step 11 Cultivate Support

Step 12 Resolicit for Support

E. Make a transition into need, i.e., "Because of your interest, I am writing to see whether you'd like to be part of my team."

F. Specific need—"As you may know, part of my responsibility is to . . . "

G. Discuss how the need will be met. "While I'm back in _____, I'm meeting with interested individuals to find those who would like to join me as part of my financial support team. Because I'm unable to visit with you personally, I'm writing to give you an opportunity to be involved."

H. Challenge; ask specifically. "Will you prayerfully consider helping at this time with a monthly commitment of $30 to $35?"

I. Express appreciation and close.

J. "P.S. I look forward to talking with you." The P.S. will probably be the first thing the individual reads. It is best to handwrite it.

Outline for a Support Raising Letter to Someone You've Never Met

A. How I got your name and why I'm writing to you

B. Personal
1. How I came to know Christ (in a nutshell)
2. How I became acquainted with the mission
3. How God led me to be on staff

C. Ministry
1. What I am doing
2. My personal vision
3. How my ministry fits in with the goals of the mission

D. As you may know . . . (partnership aspect of ministry)

E. How the need will be met ("I'm writing to ask you . . .")

F. Challenge ("Will you . . . ")

G. Thank again and express appreciation ("I will be calling you . . ."—give time frame —"in about a week")

H. "P.S. I look forward to talking with you."

Sample Letter to a Referral

[Date]

Dear Mr. & Mrs. Ladd,

Recently, I was speaking with a mutual friend, Howard Kern, and he suggested that I contact you.

Currently I am in the process of joining the missionary staff of Inner City Impact in Chicago.

Two years ago, my college roommate challenged me to attend a weekly Bible study with her, and I saw my need for Christ. I accepted Him as my personal Savior.

My life changed radically. I began to attend church and grew spiritually. Eventually I served in the church's youth ministry with the teens.

One day I had occasion to speak with a missionary who visited our church. I was impressed by his dedication, and before I knew it God began to tug at my heart. To make a long story short, I made application and was accepted as a missionary with Inner City Impact.

Inner City Impact has two focuses: evangelism and discipleship. In a five-block radius from our center, there are 10,000 young people. What a mission field! They are black, hispanic, and anglo, and each is in need of God's love.

ICI assigned me to the Humboldt Park community where I will work with inner city teens. I look forward to seeing them saved and discipled.

My vision is to see some of these teens complete high school, go to college, and eventually get married and establish Christian homes.

Inner City Impact requires that I raise my entire salary. That in itself is quite a challenge, but I look forward to building a team of loyal supporters who will give financially and lift me up in prayer.

Because I would love to have you as a member of my team, I ask that you prayerfully consider supporting me at $50 per month.

Thanks so much for your consideration. I will plan to call you in about a week to see if I can answer any further questions and to learn of your decision.

Meanwhile, the Lord bless. Have a great week in the Lord!

Sincerely,

Dolly Cruz

Adding a P.S.

A writer gets 1.5 times more positive response (support) by adding a P.S. than he would if he did not add it.[2] Following is a sample P.S.

> P.S. Because of the urgency of the need to report to my assignment, I will attempt to give you a call in a week to hear your decision.

In the P.S. the word *attempt* is used. That is an appropriate word because you may be unable to get the phone number or unable to reach them for another reason.

And remember that a handwritten P.S. is more effective than a typed one.

Some of the following notes on writing letters are from the Campus Crusade.[3]

Notes on Letter Writing

Use correct grammar, but write in an easy-flowing, conversational manner.

Keep words, sentences, and paragraphs short. Sentences should not exceed twenty-eight words and should average twelve words. Another way to check your length is through the Rule of "6": six letters or less to a word; sixteen words or less to a sentence; six sentences or less to a paragraph. Shorter paragraphs enhance the readability of the copy. Avoid unnecessary words—cut ruthlessly as if you were an editor.

Double-space between paragraphs.

Indent paragraphs for greater readability and personalization. If you have a second page, divide a sentence at the end of page 1 so that the reader will turn to page 2 to finish reading the sentence.

Be simple, not complex. Keep sentence structure uncomplicated. Guard against using incomplete sentences.

Use familiar words and correct spelling. When in doubt, look it up. Write the way you talk.

Use active not passive verbs. Look for passive verbs that you can make active. Invariably, that will produce a shorter sentence, which is preferable. "The cherry tree was chopped down by George Washington" (passive verb, nine words). "George Washington chopped down the cherry tree" (active verb, seven words).

Avoid beginning a sentence, especially the first sentence of a paragraph, with *a, an,* or *the.* Begin sentences with action words (verb forms such as "ing" words) or good transitions (such as prepositional phrases) to keep the interest of the reader and to enhance the flow from one thought to another.

Avoid beginning a paragraph with "I." Vary paragraph beginnings.

Use a personal form for your letter. That means using a comma after the salutation rather than a colon and not using an inside address (the addressee's address).

Use concrete words that your reader can visualize. Abstract words dull your writing. Add variety. Develop your own personal style.

Always give your letter a specific date.

Write to express—not to impress. Your letter should flow from the general to the specific. Narrow your focus, thinking of it as a funnel. Tie your letters to your reader's experience. Proceed from the known to the unknown.

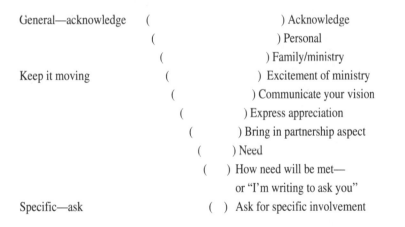

```
General—acknowledge    (                    ) Acknowledge
                        (                    ) Personal
                        (                    ) Family/ministry
Keep it moving          (                    ) Excitement of ministry
                        (                    ) Communicate your vision
                        (                    ) Express appreciation
                        (                    ) Bring in partnership aspect
                        (    ) Need
                        (  ) How need will be met—
                            or "I'm writing to ask you"
Specific—ask            (  )  Ask for specific involvement
```

Understand that this is a very specific letter, with the goal of raising funds. It should not be confused with the monthly prayer letter that is a more general tool to communicate, encourage, update, and share prayer requests. This letter should focus on your financial need.

Things to Avoid When Writing Support Need Letters

When writing a letter for monthly support or special needs—maternity, a car, medical, or other expenses—be careful of the following weaknesses.

Never write about your deficit. Any deficit you have is made up of identifiable needs. Therefore, write about needs to which the reader can relate—medical expenses, auto expenses, special training expenses, and so on. Note the basic categories on your reimbursement form. These are needs that can be explained, but never do so in deficit terms.

Never ask a person to give to your general budget. The giver needs to know that his gift helps you and makes a difference. Allow the one you ask to be a partner in meeting an identifiable need to enable you to carry out your ministry objective. Giving to a general budget need is like throwing a pebble onto a rock pile—the element of identification is lost. Your "general budget" is made up of many identifiable parts, so raise the parts that point to success and accomplishment.

Never apologize for writing or calling a person whom you wish to involve in meeting a need. You are providing an opportunity for him to minister through his resources. Remember, the giver needs to give far more than any cause needs to receive a gift. When you apologize, you appear to be a beggar rather than a child of the King.

Never ask for a general amount, for a general reason, and without a time frame in which to take action. You should challenge people to a specific gift amount, or at least give them a specific range. When you have a definite deadline you're working toward, mention it in your letter.

Never promise to call without calling. Always follow through on your commitment.

Never send so many personal letters at once that it is impossible to keep your commitment of following up with a phone call to each person.

Follow-up Phone Call

To this point you have given it your best shot with the personal letter. Now comes the most critical part—the follow-up phone call. The phone call will provide that much needed two-way conversation.

Identify yourself and chat briefly (3-5 minutes) with the individual. Ask a sincere question, such as, "How are you and your family doing?" Be sure to listen and respond as needed.

Ask if he or she received your letter. Be ready to respond appropriately. The following could happen:

1. He hasn't received it.

2. He received it but hasn't read it.

3. He looked at it but can't remember the details.

4. He has read it and has made a decision.

When any of the first three takes place, be prepared to explain your need over the phone. Do not offer to send another letter. Be bold, and ask over the phone. Sometimes you may need to call back for the decision. But usually it will be made while you are on the phone. Be sure to try to get a commitment for an exact amount. That confirms the commitment in his mind, and it helps you in your planning process.

When appropriate, ask for prayer requests.

Your conversation might go something like this:

"As you can sense by my letter, we are looking for friends that believe in our ministry and are willing to support us through their prayers and their gifts. Would you be willing to support us at $25 per month?"

Remember they will come back to you with one of four responses:

Response 1: "Yes, I would be glad to support you at $ xxx."

Response 2: "No, we are unable to support you at that level."

Response 3: " We need some time to review our commitments and pray about this matter. I don't believe we can give you an answer tonight."

Response 4: "We cannot provide either a pledge or a special gift."

Do review how to answer these responses by referring back to Chapter 13, Step 6-*Conduct the Visit*.

Thank him for his decision. Even if the decision is no, thank him for his prayerful consideration.

Don't forget to write a thank you letter (see chapter 15).

There is no question that the letter/phone strategy will work, but much depends on how you work this plan. It takes discipline to send letters systematically and to write a date on the calendar when you plan to place the follow-up call. Your friends will be excited to hear your voice and equally excited to hear more about your plans for missionary service.

1. *Identify the prospects whom you will not be able to visit personally to ask for support._____*

_____

2. *Prioritize that list by high, medium, and low.*

3. *Choose one person, and imagine that you have ten minutes to visit with him or her. What will you say?_____*

_____

4. *Finalize a letter to ask for support from those whom you will not be able to visit personally.*

5. *Send letters to your high-priority people. (Remember not to send out so many letters at one time that you are not able to follow up effectively by phone.)*

6. *Role-play your phone follow-up script.*

7. *When asking over the phone if a prospect received your letter, be ready to respond appropriately to the following scenarios. How will you respond to each?*

> *He hasn't received it.*
> *He received it but hasn't read it.*
> *He looked at it but can't remember the details.*
> *He has read it and made a decision.*

1. *Complete the exercises under Self-Guided Training.*

2. *Read and critique one another's letters. Discuss the positive aspects and offer suggestions for improvements.*

3. *Role-play your phone scripts for the group and in groups of two.*

Notes

1. *Steve Rentz. New Staff Support Team Development Training Manual* Campus Crusade, 1991.
2. Mission Avaition Fellowship of Canada. *Support Team Development Student Manual* Guelph, ON:MAF, Canada, 1989.
3. *New Staff Training Manual.*

Chapter 17

It was a hot summer day, and Andy was taking a break from his support-raising activities. For weeks, things had gone very well. The Lord had met his needs, and he felt positive and upbeat. Andy had raised 10 percent of his support, then 15 percent, 20, 25, and on to 50 percent. Finally, he had 75 percent of his support raised.

But today Andy's focus was not on the 75 percent that had been pledged. He was thinking that the remaining 25 percent was still a significant amount. He asked himself, *How long will it take to raise the rest? Will I ever get to the field at this rate? Who else could he ask? Would it even be possible to raise the remaining 25 percent?*

Very few missionaries have all the contacts they need to raise support. They run out of prospects and become discouraged. Before you get stuck at a dead end, I encourage you to study three methods to get referrals.

1. Ask donors for referrals.[1]
2. Utilize the Key Man concept.
3. Conduct a dessert time.

When I look back at the growth of Inner City Impact's donor base, I see how God worked as He began to expand our network. As you study the example below, recognize that originally I only knew Paul. Because he introduced me to John, I met the others who joined our support team.

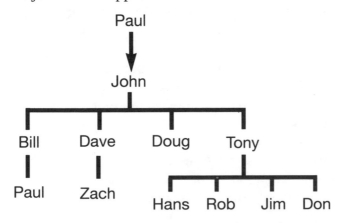

12 Step System

From Paul and especially John, an entire group of people caught the vision, one at a time. God can do the same thing in your ministry.

Asking Donors for Referrals[1]

The first method of securing referrals is to ask your donors. The Lord has given you a network of friends who can introduce you to other people in their network.

Perhaps you are already mentally identifying key donors who know you, trust you, and care for you. Whether they will help you further depends on how you have treated them. If they suffer from "donor neglect," they probably will not be willing to give referrals. But if you've loved them, cared for them, and encouraged them, they will have caught your vision and may be open to assisting you.

Those who are highly committed to you want you to be successful, and giving referrals is a way they can help. Approach your friends, and ask for names of their friends who share your burden to reach young people for Christ (or whatever target group in which you plan to minister).

Three Steps in Asking Donors for Referrals

Step 1. *Ask for names*. When collecting referrals, zero in on key areas where your donor might be able to think of names to give you. To help you do this, memorize the following dialogue using the letters *FOCUS*.

F-Friendly introduction of the referral concept.

"Thank you so much for what you are doing for me through your support and your prayers. You are very important to me. As I continue to raise support, I have sought to meet with as many people as possible. Some people have been able to participate financially whereas others have not been able to support me; yet they have had a true interest in my ministry."

O-Opening question.

"One thing I recognize is that my contacts are limited. I am wondering if you could assist me. Can you introduce me to some friends who share our common vision?" In several words state that vision, i.e., "Our common vision is to see young people come to Christ."

example, do not say, "Our common vision is to see inner city young people come to Christ." The danger is that some might respond saying, "I can't say I know of anyone who has talked about being specifically interested in inner city young people." Make the vision statement more broad: "Our vision is to see young people come to Christ."

At this point do not pause or wait for a response. Keep talking. As you continue to speak, take out a pad of paper and write your friend's name across the top. Then write numbers down the left-hand side of the sheet from one to ten to indicate that you are serious about his giving you a list of names.

C-Clarifying question.

"What are the names of your friends who share our vision?" Or, "What are the names of some of your friends who share our mutual concern about the pressures that young people today struggle with—pressures to conform to their friends' lifestyles?"

Now wait for his response. Don't panic. Wait patiently. As he responds with names, write them down. If he hesitates and can't think of anyone, go on to the next question.

U-Underscoring question.

"I know you attend First Baptist. Who are some friends there who would share our vision?"

Again, wait for the response. If he still has no names to offer, narrow the focus within the category of his church.

S-Specific questions.

Now you need to get very specific and search for sub-categories to help him surface friends on which to focus. "Tell me some of the areas in the church in which you are involved."

Focus on each area. "Who are some friends from your Sunday school class who would share the common vision you and I have?"

"Who are some friends from your weekly Bible study?"

Again, wait patiently and write down names he provides. At this point, don't worry about getting addresses and phone numbers; keep him focused on providing names.

After pursuing that category, use other categories such as: church contacts, family contacts, work contacts, club contacts, other friends, and relatives. When you have exhausted the sub-categories, proceed to Step 2.

Note: In cases where groups are mentioned, such as a Bible study, take a two-step approach: (1) Secure names from your friends, and seek to make appointments with those referrals; (2) ask to present your ministry to the group with the hope of making individual contacts for future follow-up.

Step 2. *Qualify the names.* "I am anxious to contact first those who would be most receptive to me and my vision. Whom would you recommend that I contact first? Then who?"

Place your list in front of your donor and review together the names he has just given you. Have him number them in sequence.

Next ask for addresses and phone numbers. Take careful notes on each referral. Gather basic information on each one's family, job, church, and interests.

Step 3. *Involve the donor.* "You know that I have not had a chance to meet any of these people that you have mentioned. I could use your help. Would you take several of these names and call them to arrange an appointment for the three of us sometime this week or next week? Obviously, I want to work within your schedule."

That request is your first choice. But if your friend is unable or unwilling to arrange the appointment, then you need to go to one of the following options until you find one he is comfortable with.

Another option is to have your friend set up a three-way phone conversation. Your friend can introduce you by phone and bridge the gap.

In a three-way call you may feel comfortable enough to ask for a personal appointment. Ask your donor to help you stress the importance of an appointment with you.

Or perhaps your friend will call the referral in advance to indicate that he can expect a call from you. Then when you call, it will not be a cold call. He will be expecting to hear from you.

A final option is to ask your friend to send a personal letter introducing you and indicating that the referral can expect a call from you. Again you would not be making a cold call. Such a letter may look like this.

Miss Veronica Inostroza
2704 W. North Avenue
Chicago, IL 60647

Dear Veronica:
 A number of years ago Anita and I met Don Raickett. He is a quality young man, and God has

given him a very special burden for the inner city. I have kept in touch with Don and can assure you that he is going to make a difference in missions. Don has been faithfully raising his support and, I believe, has done a good job. We would like to invite you to join us in supporting Don. I have asked Don to give you a call and set up a time for you to meet him. Thanks, Veronica, for prayerfully listening to Don and his need.

Sincerely in Christ,

Nate Strand

P.S. I have enclosed an addressed and stamped envelope. If you decide to join his support team, your gift may be mailed in this cnvclopc. Checks should be made out to "Outreach, International."

Be sure to follow up on every name you receive.

Scanning Directories for Referrals

One effective way to build a list of prospects is to go through church, club, or community directories with people. Leafing through a list of names will jog your friend's memory and is a good way to build your own list of names. Again, you need to memorize the dialogue using the letters FOCUS. You'll notice that the following dialogue is the same as for asking friends for referrals in F and O. The approach is changed slightly, beginning with C—Clarifying Question.

Step 1. *Get names.*

F-Friendly introduction of the referral concept.

"Thank you for what you are doing for me through your support and your prayers. As I continue to raise support, I have sought to meet with as many people as possible. Some people have been able to participate financially whereas others have not been able to support me; yet they have had a true interest in my ministry."

O-Opening question.

"I recognize that my contacts are limited, and I wonder if you could assist me. Can you introduce me to some friends who share our common vision?" Those questions should be stated rhetorically. Do not pause for a response.

C-Clarifying question.

"If you're like me, it's hard to come up with names right off the top of your head. But I have found that looking through a church or club directory helps bring names to mind. If you have a church directory, would you mind if we took a few minutes to go through it together?"

Some people might be reluctant to share names from a directory. Reassure them that you will not use the whole directory, but you know that it will help to identify individual friends who share your vision for the Lord's work.

U-Underscoring names.

"Great, let's just take a quick look through it together. And I'll underline the names that you identify."

Open the directory. To help surface people, you might suggest sub-categories, i.e., "Who are friends that are in your Sunday school class or in the youth ministry at your church? Which of the people here on the first page do you think would share our common vision?"

S-Specific follow-through.

"Would you mind if I borrowed your directory overnight so I can make a copy of the names we have checked?"

Reassure your donor that you will contact only those names he or she has listed.

If your donor will allow you to use the directory for a longer period of time, that may be helpful for you to contact others from the same church. They, too, could look through your copy and identify some of their friends.

Wait for a response. If he is unwilling to lend his directory, copy down the names on a sheet of paper.

Step 2. *Qualify the names.* Use the same dialogue here as in "Asking Donors for Referrals."

Step 3. *Involve your donor.* Follow the same dialogue and options as under "Asking Donors for Referrals."

Qualifying Precompiled Lists

Another effective strategy for getting referrals is to compile lists of names within people groups (doctors, lawyers, teachers, and so on) and then to ask individuals to qualify them.

Step 1. *Get names.* The most obvious source for you is the church directory. In the last script we talked about photocopying the church directory. If you do that you should tell your friend who allows you to copy his directory that you would like to show the list to others so they can identify those who may share your vision and burden.

Another source is the yellow pages. For example, if your donor is a lawyer, you may get a list of lawyers from the yellow pages and put that list in front of him to see if he can identify friends.

Another way to compile lists is to visit your local Chamber of Commerce or library. Each has published directories of businesses and professional associations. You might copy down the names on the directory posted in the lobby of the medical group where your doctor's office is located and have your family physician qualify the list of those with whom he works.

Step 2. *Qualify the names.* After you have compiled a list, use this suggested script.

"I have been able to secure this list of [doctors] in your area. I could really use your help. Who on this list do you think I should talk with first?"

Step 3. *Involve your donor in the contact.* Follow the procedure recommended in Step 3 under "Asking Donors for Referrals."

Calling Referrals for the Appointment

When you call a referred person, introduce yourself as follows.

Begin by identifying yourself. "This is Bill Dillon from Inner City Impact in Chicago. Is Tammy Schulz in?"

Make sure you have the right person. Remember you need to decide in the case of couples which one you want to talk to.

Talk about the person who made the reference. "A mutual friend of ours, Sherry Hervey, thought it would be wise for me to contact you. I really have appreciated Sherry. She has been a big help to me, and she certainly speaks highly of you. She has quite a heart for the Lord and missions. How long have you known Sherry?"

Talk about the referral. "Sherry indicates that you are a doctor. How long have you been practicing?"

"Sherry mentioned you are a member of First Baptist. How

long have you been attending the church? I understand you teach a Sunday school class."

If you feel comfortable ask about her family or work.

State the reason you are calling. "Perhaps Sherry has told you that I am planning to serve as a missionary. I would like to meet with you and explain more of the details of my ministry and the vision the Lord has given me."

Ask for the appointment. "I would like to meet with you for about twenty to thirty minutes. Would it be better this week or next week?"

Finalize details. "That's great. I will plan to see you at 6:00 P.M. next Friday, September 17, at your home. Your home address is 2251 Pine—is that correct? Will you give me directions from the Kennedy Expressway?"

Wrap up your conversation. "I'm looking forward to being with you. See you next Friday."

With a busy businessperson you probably will not have time to engage in small talk. In that case, move more quickly to asking for the appointment.

In handling phone objections review chapter 12 on making appointments.

It would be wise to send a letter confirming the appointment, especially if it is more than a week in advance. Write the reminder letter the day the appointment is made. The letter should be neatly handwritten on personal or nice stationery. Never send a printed or form letter.

[Date]

Dear Tammy,

I enjoyed talking with you on the phone today, and I appreciate your desire to reach young people for Christ. I am anxious to share my excitement and involvement in this ministry.

We live in a time when many forces are battling for the minds of young people and the challenge of sharing God's Word is tremendous. I know you will be encouraged by what we are doing in this regard.

Thanks again for your interest. I look forward to meeting you on Friday, September 17 at 6:00 P.M. at your home.

Expanding Your Contact List Through a Key Man

Campus Crusade offers the following pointers on this concept of identifying a Key Man.[2]

The key man (or woman) is usually a successful businessperson in a community other than your own whom you ask to act in your behalf in raising your support. It also may be an older Christian man or woman who has retired.

Benefits of Using a Key Man

You can make more efficient use of your time by having a key man arrange contacts and eliminate conflicts before you arrive in an area.

Because the key man is in the business community, he'll be able to open doors and secure appointments that you might not be able to make.

Relying on a local key person decreases your cost of long-distance support development as he makes the phone calls and handles activities locally.

As you train your key man, you can pour your life into him and then ask him to select someone else he could bring along to assist him, thereby giving you two key men in a given area.

The greatest benefit for the key man is his spiritual growth. As he prays, plans, and works with you, his faith will increase and his relationship with Christ will be strengthened. He will play a direct role in reaching people for Christ as he helps you develop support for your ministry.

Choosing the Key Man

Ask yourself, *Who is interested in my ministry and would help me develop my support?* Check the list of professional people who have known you in the past and who would give time to help you. Be receptive to a name God might impress on your mind.

Brief your key man thoroughly
• on the ministry of your mission.
• on your personal testimony.
• on your purpose and ministry.

Specific Ways Your Key Man Can Help
A. Support you financially.
B. Pray for you daily.
C. Give you referrals.
D. Write letters of introduction.
E. Call for appointments.
F. Go with you to appointments.
G. Set up group meetings.
H. Sponsor a dessert time or home meeting.
I. Follow up some of your contacts during the year.

Remember, you will always be looking for people to add to your support list. So use the above tools to secure additional referrals and continue reading to learn how to expand contacts through a dessert time or home meeting (see chapter 18).

The Lord has people out there, but He depends on you to go out and find them. The dessert time can help you find them.

Expand Contacts Through a Dessert Time

A dessert time is when a donor invites friends to his home, prepares a dessert, and you present your ministry. It can take many different forms. And although I use the term "dessert time," it could be a luncheon, for men only, women only, or for couples. It could be held at a country club, a home, or a business club. Let your imagination run wild. Your goal is to put your ministry in front of new people.

Several years ago I asked one of our donors to gather friends for a dessert time. Although I was disappointed by the low turnout, I was very excited about presenting the ministry of ICI. That was the night that I met a young couple who became interested in our ministry. They made an initial gift to the ministry. Through the years they have continued to give and have increased their giving. I learned that dessert times are worth it.

The Planning Process
Planning means answering several questions: Why? Where? Who? What? When? How much?

Why? The goal of the dessert time is to expose new people to your ministry. Pray that some eventually will become donors.

Where? The typical response to this question is to have the dessert time in the home of your donor. But keep an open mind.

Some donors may want to meet at a club, use a conference room at their business, or use a banquet room. Let the host make the choice.

How many? You probably should not have more than twenty guests. If you have more than that, you lose the personal touch. But do invite twice as many as you expect to attend.

Who should sponsor the dessert time? A trusted donor who knows you, trusts you, cares for you, and has invested financially in your support. Remember, the greater the involvement of a donor, the greater his commitment to you. Hosting a dessert time (or luncheon) involves your donor in your ministry in a significant way. Remember, high-priority donors attract other high-priority donors.

Who should be invited? Convey to your host or hostess some basic criteria. For example: "The specific kind of person I would like to meet is . . ."

A. Someone who would be excited about what God is doing here and around the world in terms of (identify a specific aspect of your ministry).

B. Someone who is able to support God's work through prayer and finances.

Several days before the event, ask the host or hostess to give you a complete guest list. Study the list so that you are familiar with the names. If the hostess does not give you the list before the event, arrive early so you can study the list.

Try to obtain the following information about each person attending: name of husband/wife, full address, home phone, office phone, occupations, home church, and other background information.

If the host thinks it's necessary, you can call each invited guest yourself. Tell each one how much you look forward to meeting him or her, explain the evening's program, and say you're looking forward to whatever he is bringing. (You can find that out from the host.)

What should be served? Keep the menu simple, but let your host or hostess decide. If he wants to make it a dinner party, that's his choice.

When should the dessert time take place? There is no right or wrong answer, but there are a few don'ts.

1. Don't schedule a dessert time during a holiday season.

2. Don't schedule it when it will conflict with other special events, for example, a church concert.

3. Don't schedule it too early in the evening when people are still commuting from their offices.

What kind of dessert time is it? It is an informational meeting. There will be no fund-raising, offering, or pledges taken. It is critical that your host convey this to potential guests.

After stressing several times to my host that the dessert time would be solely informational, I was asked again as I was setting up, "Bill, you will not be asking for funds, is that correct?" I reassured my host that I would not.

Part of the reason for that is that you cannot challenge a group to do anything. Groups do not make decisions. Individual people make decisions. You will be far more effective doing individual follow-up.

What should the schedule be? Here is a sample schedule for an evening dessert time that you may adapt to your situation.

6:15.   Arrive early to set up, talk with your host, and seek any last-minute advice that he might have. Go through the guest list once more.

If you are showing a multimedia presentation or video, plan in advance to have a screen or TV, extension cord, three prong plug, and so on. Obviously you need to arrive early enough to set up. You should be relaxed as you greet people, not disorganized and hurrying around.

7:00.   Guests arrive. Introduce yourself to each person. A warm smile and a friendly handshake will create a good first impression.

Let the host start when he or she feels comfortable. He might want to wait for certain key people before beginning. Your host should make sure that everyone has been introduced.

7:15-7:20. When the host feels the time is right, he welcomes the group, makes opening comments, and gives his endorsement of you and your ministry. New people will rely on their friend's endorsement. But be sensitive. Some people are more skilled and comfortable in leading a group than others. Ask the host to prepare his comments prayerfully and to enthusiastically endorse your ministry.

7:20-7:30.   You give a brief personal testimony. If the host/hostess doesn't say anything about his relationship with you, you can do this at the beginning of your presentation. State how much you appreciate him or her.

7:30-7:45.   Give your multimedia or slide presentation (if applicable).

7:45-8:00.   Talk about your vision and burden. Tell the story of one person who has been affected by your ministry, and paint a word picture of that person.

8:00-8:05. Close. Touch on your support goal, but do not ask for money. Rather, say that in the future you would welcome the opportunity to explain your vision more specifically and to talk about how guests might play a role in your ministry.

8:05. End with a question and answer session, but don't let it drag. As you close, distribute literature from your ministry, a prayer card, or prayer letter.

8:10. Dessert.

Talk with each guest personally, and thank him or her for coming. Attempt to set an appointment with key prospects before they leave. Have your calendar in hand, and strike while the iron is hot. People can lose their enthusiasm so it's important to follow up on the spot.

After everyone has left, help the host clean up, and sincerely thank him for all that he has done. Before you leave, debrief with the host and ask what feedback he received from the guests. Take the guest list out, and review it name by name. Ask who the host considers to be high-priority prospects.

What should I do in the way of follow-up? Once you leave, record whatever information you can recall about each guest. If you have a portable hand-held dictation machine or tape recorder, record your information on the way home. If you are married, one of you can make notes while the other drives.

The more you know, the more it could help you in the future. Below is a sample list of items to add to your notes about the guests.

Children's names and ages
Hobbies
Prayer requests
Hometown
Career(s)
If owners of his/her own company, product,
   profit, and competition
Names of other ministries they support
Giving patterns—Do they give monthly? Quarterly?
   Or at the end of the year?
How much do they give?
How do they give? Does she give stock? Does he give
   through his church?
Kinds of projects he likes to support

189

Kinds of projects she does not support
Names of future prospects
Churches each has attended
Names of mutual friends
Name of missions chairman at his church
Organizations to which she belongs

Listen, listen, listen. Then write it down.

Within twenty-four hours, send a personal letter of thanks to the host and to each guest. State in the letter that you would like to stay in touch with them and that you will send them an update on your ministry from time to time. That is a nice touch that says, "I am putting you on my mailing list."

Rank each guest for follow-up as an "H" for high-priority prospect, an "M" for medium-priority prospect, or an "L" for a low-priority prospect. The highs warrant a personal call to ask for an appointment. The mediums also should get a phone call. The lows are sent a letter according to the letter/phone strategy described in step 9 (see chapter 16).

Because the host has given you the names and addresses of the guests, you can add these names to your mailing list. You do not need people to sign up for your prayer letter during the dessert time.

Bathe your planning in prayer, get an early start, and have fun as you build new relationships.

Commonly Asked Questions

Some questions a host/hostess might ask are:

Will you ask for money?

No, the dessert time is to be informational only. We will not take an offering or ask people to give. We want them to meet us, and then we want to encourage their interest.

Whom do you specifically suggest I invite?

A. Someone who would be excited about what God is doing here and around the world in terms of (identify a specific aspect of your ministry).

B. Someone who is able to support God's work through prayer and finances.

Use the following checklist to build a guest list:

1. Church contacts. Go through your church directory, and add your friends to your list. Also think of people you have met through special groups such as Sunday school, Bible studies, care groups, committees, boards, and so on.

2. Relatives
3. Neighbors
4. Friends at work
5. Club and civic group contacts (contacts from groups as PTA, Rotary, Kiwanis, Lions, Optimist)
6. Friends—review your Christmas list and address book

What do you expect me as host to do?

Make a guest list.

Set a date.

Provide a place to meet.

Invite the guests approximately twenty-one days before the dessert time.

Arrange for equipment to show the video.

Mail me a copy of the guest list.

Provide a dessert.

What will take place at the dessert time?

I will arrive forty-five to sixty minutes before the starting time to review the guest list with you, answer questions you have, and set up video or multimedia presentation.

I will greet visitors as they arrive.

You will make a simple introduction to the group.

I will give my presentation.

The evening will conclude with serving dessert.

Conducting a Dessert Time Out of Town

Schedule a dessert time during the first part of your trip to another city or state. That will allow time to follow up with appointments during the remainder of your visit. Following is a sample schedule to maximize a dessert time out of town.

1. Saturday—Conduct a dessert time.

2. Sunday—Be present in the church. If possible, take part in the service: preach, give a brief report, or speak to a Sunday school class.

3. Monday—Set appointments.

4. Monday and Tuesday—Attend appointments.

Following is a variation on the dessert time which Wycliffe calls home meetings. The first thing you want to do is choose a host or hostess and send a letter similar to the following.

[Date]

Dear _____,

In a couple of months we'll drive up the coast to visit many of our friends and relatives. Joan and I would enjoy visiting with you. We'll never forget the last time! You sure know how to make folks feel at home.

Would it be possible to stay with you again? The kids like sleeping in their sleeping bags, so they don't need any special place.

You'll probably remember from our last newsletter that we still have a way to go to reach the monthly budget Wycliffe has set for us. In fact, that's the reason for this trip. We can't leave for our assignment until the financial requirement is met.

Several friends like you are already financial and prayer partners. Others said they will start within the next few weeks. But we still need to see the Lord provide more partners. We're asking a few friends to think about helping us in a different and special way through a home meeting.

Two families have already let us know they are going to invite their acquaintances for a potluck evening. That will give them a chance to introduce us to their friends. We'll present the challenge of Bible translation from the standpoint of recruiting others to join the translation team.

We've been thinking of ways to meet more people so we can make known the wonderful things God is doing through Bible translation. Would you consider hosting a home meeting? An outline of a typical meeting is enclosed. It states each of our responsibilities.

We'll call in one week to talk with you about our staying with you and your decision regarding a home meeting. Should you have other ideas you'd like us to try, please share them with us. We're open to almost anything.

Would you put our trip and our need for more partners on your prayer calendar? Your faithful praying has always been an encouragement. Thanks!

Follow-up Telephone Call to Host/Hostess

After you've sent the letter explaining the home meeting concept, call each potential host in a week. It is possible that your friends will not be comfortable with the idea of a dessert time or that they have other reasons for not helping in this way.

The friend who says no probably thinks he is letting you down. A good way to help him feel better is to ask him to do something else. For example, perhaps he can arrange for you to speak to his Sunday school class, meet with his missions committee, or talk with his pastor. Be sensitive and flexible.

Other friends will respond positively. When they do, confirm the date, time, and place for the meeting. Answer any questions they have after reading your letter.

It's important for you to be businesslike with your host. You may have to make more than one call to confirm the details.

Preparing for the Home Meeting

Confirm whether the host is planning a meal or a dessert. Find out if he will follow up with those invited to check that they are coming. That is particularly important when there is a length of time between the sending of the invitations and the actual event.

Contact the host/hostess one week before the scheduled meeting. Check details together to be sure the evening will run smoothly. Confirm the date, time, and place. Discuss plans and format for the evening. Ensure that the host/hostess is following up on the invitations to confirm the number of guests. Also discuss equipment needs.

Have a guest book in which each guest writes his/her name and address. You'll need that information, so you can send a thank you note to guests. If your host/hostess already has a guest book and wants to use that, copy the information in it for your records.

Mealtime is a great time for getting acquainted. If you're totally prepared, it'll be easier to relax and enjoy the evening. Check on last-minute details while your host/hostess is cleaning and straightening up.

Do all you can to help your host be successful. Pray before you make each call. Ask your prayer partners to pray. Ask for their advice, and ask them to pray with you about each situation.

Host's responsibilities. Invite friends whom you think would be interested in meeting your missionary friend. If possible, invite them personally, and then follow up by sending a written invitation. Here is a sample invitation.

Bob and June Hodges
We invite you on
March 1 at 7:00 P.M.
to our home
5432 Uptown St., Downtown

This informal evening will include:
Taste Sensations
A "Pot-Bless" meal adventure
"Come By Here"
A video journey to a distant land
Intrigue
Why leave the comforts of home?
Challenge
with Bill and Bev Smith
We'll contact you soon!

Vern and Debbie Broadfield

Plan a meal so that all the invited participants will bring something. Follow up the written invitation with a personal contact to see if they plan to attend. That gives you an opportunity to work out their part in the meal.

Introduce the missionary to the group. Tell something about how you came to know him/her and why you think it's important for them to become acquainted with the mission organization and the missionary. If you are a prayer or financial partner, it's helpful to tell what your involvement means to you.

Your friends will be inspired by what God is doing. They will gain a better understanding of missions and will enjoy fellowship with old friends and make new friends. Christians need to be involved in something worthwhile and of eternal consequence. Some of your friends may want to be involved but don't know how.

Missionary's responsibilities. Keep accurate records. Details can get blurred by a heavy schedule of meetings. Keep records of telephone calls and the details of what was discussed. Your businesslike approach in these details will mean a lot to the people who are giving their time and energies to help you.

Come prepared to make an enthusiastic presentation that includes a segment about the mission, your ministry, and how and why the members of the audience can get involved.

Provide literature for each guest. Usually that is done with a table display.

Include the host in planning all aspects of the evening.

Prepare to answer, within your range of knowledge and experience, questions from the guests.

Work out with the host a means by which each guest receives a thank you from you after the evening.

Express appreciation to the host/hostess during the meeting.

Planning Your Presentation

Even though we've been talking about the dessert time, the principles of a presentation are similar for a Sunday school class and other group settings. Keep in mind that the plan is adaptable.

Choose a film or video. It's suitable to use an audiovisual aid that shows your ministry. Select one that is suitable for the audience and which fits into the time available.

Identify with your audience. The host has already introduced you. Now it's your turn. One way to identify with your audience is by recognizing their achievements or contributions; honor them. For example, "Not every Christian cares so much about missions that he'd take time from a busy schedule to come meet a missionary he doesn't even know."

Present gift to host/hostess. Show your appreciation for the evening and all that went into the preparations. It took a lot of work and time on the part of your host/hostess. Affirm him or her.

Your personal testimony. If you have just met the guests and they have an idea of your background, give a brief testimony at this point. That establishes your credibility.

Film introduction. The following introduction could be divided between husband and wife or two partners.

"Do you know anyone who has asked a question so important that it changed the world?"

> "In the early days of this century a young man named William Cameron Townsend journeyed to Guatemala to sell Spanish Bibles to Guatemalan Indians. But

195

Townsend had a problem—the Indians couldn't read his Spanish Bibles.

"One day Townsend met an Indian man who was interested, but like all the others had no desire to own a book he couldn't read. It was this man who voiced a question—the question that was destined to change the world.

"He asked, 'If your God is so great why doesn't He speak my language?'

"I don't know what Townsend thought as he mulled over this man's question, but I know what he decided to do. He set about learning the Indian man's language, reduced it to writing, and translated the Bible into this newly written Cakchiquel language.

"It wasn't just the Cakchiqueles who got excited. Townsend got excited too. He began to realize there must be hundreds of people groups all over Latin America who never had a single word of the Bible in their own language.

"In fact as time went on, Townsend and others who began to work in this new missionary enterprise called Bible translation discovered there were about 2,500 language groups in countries all over the world who, like the Cakchiqueles, didn't have even one word of the Scriptures.

"Wycliffe is more than fifty years old now. God has led through the years and blessed in many wonderful ways. One of the great blessings is how people like us can have a part. Betty and I didn't know until 1972 that Wycliffe needed schoolteachers. When we found out, our hearts were drawn to the need and to the reality that it gave us a way of being involved directly on the mission field. We're just getting started, but we're already seeing God confirm His leading.

"We've brought a video that shows what happens to a remote group of people living in the far off hinterland of Papua New Guinea when the gospel comes to them in their own language. You'll see yourself in this film. Well, not literally. What I mean is you'll see how mission-minded believers back home were used by the Lord as partners with the missionary. The results you'll see can be attributed to joint ownership: the folks at home prayed, gave, and helped in other ways; the missionary represented them in Bible translation.

"Oh, by the way, there are two penetrating and disturbing questions asked in this film. The answers are changing the world. Listen for them. Both are asked in the last five minutes. How would you answer?"

Materials and Equipment

Prepare a last-minute checklist so that you can be sure you have everything. It's best to have all your materials and not expect the host/hostess to supply them. But accept his or her help if it is offered.

Equipment Checklist:

Projector or VCR
Screen
Take up reel
Spare projector bulb
Extension cord
Adapter plug
Partnership packets
Table display or set of materials
Other

Personal Checklist:

Name tag
Bible
Comb
Breath mints
Deodorant
Other

Plan to arrive early to set up. Don't take anything for granted. The entire evening can be ruined if equipment malfunctions.

Make sure the screen or television is placed so everyone can see it. Latecomers shouldn't have to disturb the presentation. Make a place for children if they are on the guest list.

Home Meeting Checklist
Meeting setup details
Materials:

> Handouts
> Translated New Testament
> Ballpoint pen, magic marker
> Response mechanisms
> Packets/Prayer cards
> Guest book/three-by-five cards
> Spare copies of scripts

On the scene:

> Get there early
> Go over equipment
> Check room, seating, ventilation
> Refreshments
> Host/Hostess gift

Follow up:

> Record biographical information on three-
>   by-five cards
> Turn in media and equipment (if rented)
> Turn in blue card to regional offices
> Thank you cards to the host and attenders
> Short note to those who could not attend
>   and perhaps some follow-up for these few
> Record the responses gathered
> Develop a plan of action for each attender[3]

Dessert times can be fun. They reinforce your donor's commitment to you and give you introductions to new people. A dessert time does not take a lot of time and energy to pull off; the real work comes in your follow-up.

Perhaps you had come to a dead end in your support raising. I trust this chapter has given you hope because you will be amazed at the number of new people whom God wants to bring to your team.

1. *Memorize and role-play with another person how to ask a friend for referrals.*

2. *Memorize and role-play with another person how to check a directory for referrals with a friend.*

3. *Memorize and role-play with a friend how to qualify a precompiled list with a friend.*

4. *Role-play with another person how to call referrals for an appointment.*

5. *Identify three high-priority donors whom you would like to ask for a referral.* _____

_____

6. *Call or visit with those three high-priority donors, and ask them for referrals. Don't forget to involve your donor in helping you get that appointment.*

7. *Identify three donors who might serve as key people for you. Prioritize them and ask for their commitment.*

_____

_____

8. *Gather some friends and do a mock dessert time.*

1. *Break into groups and practice the steps above.*

2. *Choose people who will role-play each step in front of the entire group. Other members of the group take notes and critique the role-plays.*

3. *For maximum training, place a call to a donor, and ask for referrals in the presence of your instructor.*

4. *Conduct a dessert time in the classroom or, for the real effect, go into someone's home.*

5. *Follow the steps given to identify high-priority donors, and invite them to host dessert times.*

Notes

1. Referral material adapted from "How to Get Hundreds and Hundreds of Support Contacts" by Frank C. Dickerson, copyright 1990. Used by permission. For further information contact The Ministry Leadership Group, 7412 Club View Drive, Highland, CA 92346. Phone (909)864-2798; Fax (909)864-2494.
2. Crusade Key Man concept—Steve Rentz.
3. This letter and the rest of this chapter have been adapted from materials from Wycliffe Bible Translators. Used by permission.

Chapter 18

Andy had been on the field for more than a year. One day he sat down to review his support. When he brought his records up to date, he learned that Mr. Kern had stopped giving six months before. Liz Stern, another supporter, had quit giving also. No wonder Andy was not receiving his full support.

When I first entered missions, I assumed that support raising was a one-time event because I failed to consider the loss of donors. People die, their incomes fall, and their giving interests change.

In the seventies, a hot button for evangelical giving was Vietnamese refugees. That was followed by food for the starving in Africa. With the tearing down of the Iron Curtain, giving attention turned to the newly open doors of the Eastern European countries.

Times change, and people's giving habits change as well. Most missionaries must keep their ministry before supporters, and support cultivation—the keeping of support—is an ongoing issue.

Support cultivation is comparable to a farmer cultivating his field. He doesn't throw seed on the field and then leave it there. He prepares the ground, plants, fertilizes, waters, and weeds. As a result of hours of hard work, the farmer expects a good crop.[1] A missionary, too, must work his field by staying close to those who are currently supporting him to keep them on his team.

The missionary who doesn't cultivate his support may use one of the following excuses:[2]

"I hate to write letters."
"I'm not the thank-you type."
"People don't expect personal notes."
"I don't have the money for stationery and gifts."
"I'm too busy."
"I don't care."
"I cannot write good letters."

If you neglect your donors
- they will find another place to invest.
- they will not consider your ministry a priority. If it were a priority, wouldn't you communicate that to them?

Step 11:
Cultivate Support

12 Step System

201

- their commitment to you will decrease. They may not actually drop your support, but they will remain less than totally involved.
- they will not be as willing to give you referrals. They will not want you to treat their friends the way you treat them.

"The largest share of customer (and donor) attrition is actually a cost of doing business poorly. Out of every 100 individuals who stop supporting you:

"You cannot abuse people and expect them to help you."

four move away or die.

fifteen have made a decision that another organization can serve them better.

fifteen are unhappy with your organization (and telling others that).

sixty-six think you don't care about them."[3]

What Is Cultivation?

"You cannot abuse people and expect them to help you," says Steve Rentz of Campus Crusade. He goes on to say that cultivation is not merely sending prayer letters to inform your ministry partners of your activities. It entails more than simply "reporting in" on monthly news or prayer requests. "Cultivation is the process of developing and communicating warmth and concern for your people. This involves a commitment to build relationships with your ministry partners just as you would build relationships with those in your field of ministry."[4] Support cultivation is ministry, and you should view your donors as part of a team, as your ministry partners.

"The Bible frequently exhorts believers to thank God for all things. It is a Christ-like characteristic to be thankful to God and people."[5]

> *With my mouth I will greatly extol the Lord; in the great throng I will praise him. (Ps. 109:30)*
> *I have not stopped giving thanks for you, remembering you in my prayers. (Eph. 1:16)*
> *Let the peace of Christ rule in your hearts, since as members of one body you were called to peace. And be thankful. (Col. 3:15)*

Support cultivation is a process, a lifetime ministry.

Adding Value

Once a salesperson sells a product, the transaction is over. The commodity changes hands, and payment is made. But good salespeople add something to the value already traded. That can mean showing a personal interest; a real estate agent might phone or drop by after closing on a home to ask how the new homeowner is settling in. The salesperson of a photocopier may, after the sale, include some supplies at no charge. The point is that the extra is unexpected and unrequested; it is a value added to the sale.

Your support team has expectations: they are interested in—and entitled to—information about your ministry. Some of those expectations are tied into their reasons for giving. In addition, they expect prayer letters, personal visits, reports, and so on. Every contact you make with a supporter bonds him to you and your ministry and increases his interest in you.

When you give a tangible gift to a supporter, the results may be quite unexpected. Of course you do not give a gift for the purpose of receiving something in return; you give it because you love and appreciate your supporting team member. But your gift could generate prayer. It may generate more financial support. It could be the "gentle" nudge the Lord uses to propel another worker to the field. If nothing else, the gift will increase the sense of family and teamwork that you are trying to generate.

Caring for Donors

This outline lists attitudes and perspectives necessary in showing appropriate care for your donors.[6]

1. **Incorrect attitudes**
   a. Viewing the support team as an inconvenience or added responsibility that consumes your time
   b. Desiring to get by as inexpensively as possible
      1) Not corresponding regularly because of the cost of postage
      2) Using inferior paper for prayer letters
      3) Thinking that small gifts aren't practical
   c. Assuming your support team is not concerned about you
   d. Seeing your support team only in a financial

perspective

2 . Correct attitudes

    a. Viewing team members as friends rather than as financial investors

    b. Depending on the character of God, realizing that He, the faithful One, provides for our financial support

    c. Endeavoring to be open and personal with your team

    d. Seeking to be generous with your time and money to cultivate your support team

3. Steps

    a. Pray for your partners—outline an organized way to pray for your support team. Decide how you will share prayer requests and answers with one other. Ask about answers the next time you see/talk to them.

    b. Communicate love.

        1) Help with their psychological needs

            a) Help people feel needed

            b) Help people feel appreciated

            c) Help them feel a part of what you are doing

        2) Help with spiritual needs

            a) Their walk with God

            b) Growth and understanding of God's Word

            c) Understanding God's will for their lives

    c. Communicate regularly—set a communication calendar/plan.

    d. Maintain a personal communication record.

    e. Maintain a year-end investment record.

    f. Develop an information file on your supporters. It is an ongoing process.

    g. Don't overlook children and other family members. Maintain a family network.

Communicating with Donors

How can you build a bond with your donors? What is the most effective way to maintain communication?

Let's review the Harvard list of communication tools ranked by effectiveness. This should be your starting point as you cultivate your support.

1. One-on-one contacts
2. Small group discussion
3. Large group discussion
4. Telephone
5. Handwritten letter
6. Typed letter
7. Mass letter
8. Newsletter
9. Brochure
10. News item
11. Advertisement
12. Handout

Do what is practical. Using the above list, write down ways you can communicate with supporters in the order of their effectiveness.

Visit Your Key Donors on One-on-One

You may not have an opportunity to visit until your next home leave, but for some missionaries special trips back to the States make this a viable option. The point is that this is the most effective means of cultivating support.

I set appointments regularly to take donors out for a meal, which is a very good use of my time and theirs.

Visit with Your Donors in a Small Group Setting

If a number of donors live in a given geographical area, ask one to serve as your host and invite several others over for an evening. Although it is not as good as a one-on-one visit, this is better than a letter.

Make a Phone Call

Phoning is one of the most practical and productive means of communication. There is a cost involved, but don't be afraid to make some long-distance calls. Call during off hours, and limit the length of your conversation.

Call your high-priority donors several times a year.

Write a Personal, Handwritten Letter or Note

This is not your regular monthly prayer letter. It is a down-to-earth, personal, handwritten letter.

You may find time to write personal letters and notes when

you travel. It's been said that Josh McDowell even uses the napkins on the airplane to jot notes to his supporters.

Write a Personal Typed Letter or Note

Again, I am not talking about a prayer letter. This is a personal letter that you type.

Write a Mass Letter or Prayer Letter

This is where the regular prayer letter fits. Discipline yourself to send a prayer letter once a month. You can show appreciation more effectively by adding a personal handwritten note at the bottom of the prayer letter.

I would rather see a missionary communicate on a regular monthly basis with a straightforward prayer letter than a fancy, complicated newsletter that requires an immense amount of time and money to produce, and is sent less often. The point is to keep open the lines of communications.

Use a daily diary to help you capture and remember what you want to communicate. Plan ahead, and remember the prayer letter is not to ask for money but to keep interested people informed.

It is important for several reasons:

- To educate donors
- To deepen your relationship with them
- To enable them to pray intelligently for you; they need to be informed about answers to prayer as well as needs
- For accountability—you need people to answer to
- To increase your partnership
- To stay in front of your donors, to combat the "out of sight, out of mind" syndrome
- For ownership; donors need to feel part of your team
- To keep them informed[7]

Send a Newsletter

Nothing excites donors more than to hear that your ministry is yielding solid results. They figure their investment is worthwhile if your ministry is accomplishing what you told them it would accomplish. A well-written newsletter helps communicate that.

Three goals for the missionary newsletter:

1. Minister to your audience—bring them closer to the Lord.
2. Express appreciation.
3. Stimulate readers with your vision.[8]

The main difference between a prayer letter and a newsletter is that the newsletter has a more jazzy format. A newsletter can have headlines and short articles, a logo and special column names, such as Prayer Corner, Family News, or Village Happenings.

Let your imagination run wild. Use borders, graphics, photos, varied type fonts to add interest. You can give your newsletter a name with a logo or masthead. Note how these missionaries personalized their newsletters using their family names.[9]

The Bohm Bulletin Board
Prettos Progress
Barkey Lines
Adams Actions
Seconds with Sonya
The Gaultney Path

Evaluate a newsletter for attractiveness using these criteria.

Are paragraphs short?
Did you indent paragraphs (not block style)?
Use underlining to stop the eye.
Did you make use of white space?
Are the grammar and spelling correct?
Use dashes occasionally.
Did you use the active voice?
Use "you"—not "I." For example, "You would have enjoyed seeing . . . "
Use black ink.
Use charts, diagrams, pictures.
Keep overall visual appearance appealing. People do not read wall-to-wall writing anymore.
Circles and slanted lines tend to distract a reader.
CAPITAL LETTERS ARE HARD TO READ AND GIVE THE FEELING OF SHOUTING! Underlining is more effective.
Although you want to establish a definite layout, look for ways to vary the format and design. Use different textures and materials, pictures, graphs, and drawings.
Create a feeling of warmth in a newsletter. Catch the reader's attention by using good lead-in sentences. Talk about real people in a "you and me" style. Link paragraphs with connections: of course, however, you know, now, so you see. Keep to your point

without long paragraphs. Express appreciation.

In summary, develop a system for your newsletter. Be creative and use variety. Work on your writing skills. Develop a file of ideas.

Newsletters can be costly both in terms of money and time. In terms of communications, a newsletter is less effective than personal and prayer letters. Your goal is to communicate your love and appreciation to your donors and to give them the satisfaction that they are helping you make a difference in changing the world for Christ. You are not competing to see who has the most dramatic newsletter.

Creative Ways to Cultivate Donors

• Invite donors to the church or home at which you speak.
• Send updated family pictures.
• Write a note on the back of local product wrapper.
• When reading an article that may be of interest to a donor, cut it out or make a copy to send to him.
• Send care packages with local food products.
• Call, visit, or send a card to a donor who is sick or in the hospital.
• Send a card for a donor's birthday and anniversary.
• Send post cards and greeting cards. Consider sending cards for holidays when people don't receive many cards (Thanksgiving, Valentines, July 4). Send your annual greeting card at Thanksgiving with special thanks to them.
• Major supporters should receive a tangible token of appreciation annually. Christmas is an excellent time to send a gift—something unique from your field of ministry perhaps, or an item that will stimulate a donor's spiritual growth or prayer life.
• Send special gifts—jelly, honey, books. When you give a book, try to meet a specific need, and write a note in the flyleaf.
• Send cassette or videotapes—musical, praise, sermon, updates of your ministry. Via tape, walk donors through a day overseas—hear sounds of country, local music, and so on.
• Add to a supporter's collection of stamps, postcards, or knickknacks.
• Send small gifts from the field. Bring special gifts when home on home leave. They don't have to be expensive—be creative.
• Entertain while on home leave.
• Get to know supporters' children. Remember that a gift (i.e., Christmas tree ornaments, pictures, small games) for a supporter's

child goes a long way in deepening a relationship.

• Link up pen pals between national children and supporters' children.

• Help supporters' children on their country reports for school projects.

• Be a VBS visiting missionary.

• Set up a telephone call to the church during worship service.

• Send recipes or crafts from the field.

• Have a key representative in each church.

• Communicate who your other prayer partners are.

• I can't count the number of times I have heard pastors and mission committee members indicate that they have not heard from a missionary in months or even years. In most cases, the church has done its part, but the missionaries have chosen not to keep the communication lines open. When that happens, not only does the missionary eventually lose his support, but he has robbed individuals or churches of the satisfaction of knowing what their gifts and prayers are accomplishing.

• Stay on the lookout for additional ways to strengthen the bond between you and your supporters. Ministry partners can help strengthen the bond in the following ways.[10]

Betty Barnett in her book *Friend Raising* notes these sources which can be of help:

Mail-order-Stationery and Gifts

American Bible Society-Good selection of Scripture postcards available for $1.50 for 25 postcards (price subject to change) — Bibles and many other items excellent for discipleship and evangelism at great prices. Write for catalog: American Bible Society, P.O. Box 5656, Grand Central Station, New York, NY 10164-0851 U.S.A.

Best To You-Attractive Christian stationery and gifts through mail-order catalog. Excellent discount prices for quantity orders of 19 or more items. Write for catalog: Best to You, P.O. Box 1300, Siloam Springs, AR 72761-1300 U.S.A.

Current, Inc.-Mail-order stationery at discount prices. Includes a nice selection of Christian cards, plus a large selection of beautiful all-purpose cards, notes, and stationery. Excellent discounts for quantity orders (16 items or more). Write for catalog: Current, Inc., 1005 E. Woodmen Rd., Colorado Springs, CO 80920 U.S.A.

Delight Yourself-Handmade gift card sets, feminine and classy. Excellent discount for missionaries. Write for free sample: Jinny Rees, 4721 N. Pacific, Fresno, CA 93705 U.S.A.

Mount Carmel-"For Missionaries Only" offers Christian music tapes and books at discount prices by mail-order. For missionaries' personal use or to send as gifts to supporters. Cassette tapes are $4.25 (prices subject to change). John Michael Talbot, Twila Paris, Keith Green, Leon Patillo, Silverwind, and many others, plus a variety of classic Christian books. Send for catalog: Mount Carmel, P.O. Box 243, Leavenworth, WA 98826 U.S.A.

Prints of Peace-"Hope Kindlers for Kingdom Builders" offers catalog of Christian art, rubber stamps, and greeting cards. Provides adults and children ways to create and enliven stationery and envelopes, decorate packages and parcels, etc. Write for catalog: Prints of Peace, P.O. Box 717, Camino, CA 95709 U.S.A.

Walter Drake-Mail-order personalized address labels, stationery, mailing labels, note pads, etc. Send for catalog: Walter Drake & Sons, Drake Building, Colorado Springs, CO 80940 U.S.A.

Ways the Support Team Can Be Involved

• Pray.
• Phone periodically.
• Accompany missionary on deputation travel. That is a good time to develop friendship. Help with the mission presentation.
• Host a home meeting.
• Type/mail prayer letter—computerize mailing list and print address labels.
• Give logistical help for home leave—locate housing, car, schooling, and so on.
• Greet them at the airport.
• Help them get settled or help prepare the home for use.
• Give them a gift certificate for a special treat—at Baskin Robbins, Wendy's, or Haagen-Dazs.
• Update them on "what's in and what's out."
• Host a party in their honor and spend time praising God for His work through them. Write a litany of thanksgiving.
• Be sensitive to the length of time needed for cultural

adjustments.
- Help the kids "fit" back into homeland culture when the family comes back on home leave.
- Baby-sit for children.
- Help run errands.
- Provide meals the first days they are on home leave or the last few days before they leave.
- Plan a missionary shower. Give a food shower.
- Send the couple away for a weekend of rest just before they leave your area.
- Take them to the airport.
- Prune the shrubbery or cut the lawn during their home leave.
- Develop communication with the missionary's older parents.
- Provide money management/financial adviser with power of attorney.
- Printer—print prayer card, business card, prayer letter.
- Public speaking expert—critique church presentation.
- Media expert—produce a slide/video presentation.
- Purchase special clothes for family.
- Build crates, pack barrels, provide trucking, give storage space, or help move.
- Send a video of key North American programs/sports if missionary is out of the area.
- Send clothing or toys for nationals.
- Pack a birthday package/special "care" package—chocolate chips, salad dressing, Kool-Aid, specialty items not available in their area.
- Send church bulletins and sermon cassettes. Send church pictorial directory and address list.
- Send prayer letters of other missionaries supported by the home church.
- Send a subscription to a newspaper or articles on trends.
- Provide a gift subscription to key magazines.
- Compile a list of services and supplies needed by the missionary.
- Invite the supporting church to send a summer or short-term team to the missionary's area.
- Send books.
- Pre-address envelopes/aerograms for church members to write to missionary.
- Send party decorations and napkins for birthday parties.
- Send fashion catalogs.

In essence, develop a relationship, closeness that will keep people on your team.

• Encourage them during the emotional ups and downs.
• Learn what makes them feel supported and what the kids enjoy doing. Then do it.
• Call or visit them on the field. Write frequent letters. Send holiday cards.
• Send their favorite magazine, Sunday newspaper cartoons, candy, cereal, or Kool-Aid.
• Remember them on their birthday and holidays—send a card or gift, or call.
• Send periodic care packages to the children.
• Send a tape of worship music, sermon, greetings from the family or group of supporters.
• Write the kids individually.
• In essence, develop a relationship, closeness that will keep people on your team. Below is a real life illustration of the principle of closeness.

Our favorite illustration of closeness to the customer is car salesman Joe Girard. He sold more new cars and trucks, each year, for eleven years running, than any other human being. In fact, in a typical year, Joe sold more than twice as many units as whoever was in second place. In explaining his secret of success, Joe said: "I send out over thirteen thousand cards every month."

Why start with Joe? His magic . . . is simply service, overpowering service, especially after-sales service.

Joe's customers won't forget him once they buy a car from him; he won't let them! Every month throughout the year they get a letter from him. It arrives in a plain envelope, always a different size or color. "It doesn't look like that junk mail that is thrown out before it is opened," Joe confides. And they open it up and the front of it reads, "I like you." Inside it says "Happy New Year from Joe Girard." He sends a card in February wishing the customers a "Happy George Washington's Birthday." In March it's "Happy St. Patrick's Day." They love the cards. Joe boasts, "You should hear the comments I get on them."
Out of context, Joe's 13,000 cards sounds like just another sales gimmick. But . . . Joe seems genuinely to care. . . . Moreover, Joe has cared about every customer as

an individual. He doesn't think statistically, but emphasizes that he has sold "one at a time, face-to-face, belly-to-belly. They are not an interruption or pain in the neck. They are my bread and butter."[11]

Because of donor attrition, a missionary constantly seeks ways to add new donors to replace those who drop out. But support cultivation is not enough. Resolicitation is another important aspect of support raising.

Before moving on to resolicitation let me remind you to practice the common courtesies. Answer every letter you receive. When people do something special for you, always respond with a note of thanks. If you do not practice that common courtesy, you will lose your support.

I trust these ideas are helpful as you minister to those very special people who are your donors.

Self Guided Training

1. *Write your philosophy of support cultivation in one page.*

_____

_____

2. *If you are a veteran missionary, list specifically what you have done in support cultivation in the last ninety days. Write specifically what you will do differently in the next ninety days to improve your support cultivation.*_____

_____

_____

3. *Begin a daily diary so you are well prepared to talk about what the Lord is doing in your ministry.*

4. *What was the date you sent out your last prayer letter? What deadline are you setting for your next prayer letter? Set deadlines for your monthly prayer letters for the next six months.*_____

_____

_____

Self Guided Training

5. *List your high-priority donors, and state how you intend to communicate with them in the next ninety days. Insert the projected date under the action you will take. (These contacts are in addition to your regular monthly prayer letter.)*_____

_____

_____

6. *Reread the section "Creative Ways to Cultivate Donors," and identify three creative ideas that you will incorporate into your donor cultivation program.*_____

_____

_____

Group Guided

Training

Each member of the group should complete the exercises above. Talk together about ways to cultivate supporters.

Notes

1. Steve Rentz, *New Staff Support Team Development Training Manual.* Campus Crusade, 1991.
2. Pioneers, P.O. Box 725500 Orlando, FL 32872.
3. H. Brade and Alan J. Antin, *Secrets from the Lost Art of Common-Sense Marketing.* Chicago: Precept Press.
4. Steve Rentz, *New Staff Support Team Development Training Manual.* Campus Crusade, 1991.
5. Pioneers, P.O. Box 725500 Orlando, FL 32872.
6. Regions Beyond Missionary Union.
7. Ken Williams,Wycliffe Bible Translators.
8. Scott Morton. *Raising Personal Support: A Biblical Approach to Fund Raising.* Colorado Springs: The Navigators.
9. Wycliffe Bible Translators.
10. *Support Manual.* International Missions.
11. Thomas J. Peters and Robert H. Waterman, Jr., *In Search of Excellence* (New York: Harper & Row, 1982), 157-59.

Chapter 19

Andy felt good about his ministry on the field as well as his ongoing ministry back home in support cultivation. It was hard to gauge how successful he was, but according to what he learned by talking to and observing other missionaries, he thought he stood out above the rest, both in effective support raising and cultivation of his supporters.

Not a month went by when Andy did not receive cards and letters from supporters. And the tone of those letters told Andy that the Lord was giving them great satisfaction in giving to his ministry.

Things were going great in his relationships, but Andy realized that it had been a year since many of those supporters had made their initial pledges. During that year, many things had changed. Essye Bridgeman had been promoted, and Andy felt certain that her income capability had changed. Although Racquel Salvante initially indicated that she could not support Andy, she was now married—that might make a difference. *Now would be a good time to recontact my donors to upgrade, if possible, their pledges. I need to resolicit my supporters,* Andy thought.

A missionary should always be raising support by resoliciting current contacts. If you are a veteran missionary, there are certain to be donors on your list who are waiting to be asked again. They have given, and you have maintained contact. They believe in what you are doing and now are able to give more; they need to be resolicited.

Your home leave is an ideal time to reestablish contact and challenge your supporters to upgrade their giving. And while you are checking your donor lists, don't neglect those non-donors who now may be in a position to give.

If it is some time until your next home leave, it may be worthwhile for you to choose select donors to call and ask them by phone to upgrade their giving.

Step 12: Resolicit for Support

12 Step System

215

When diagramed, the resolicitation process looks like this:

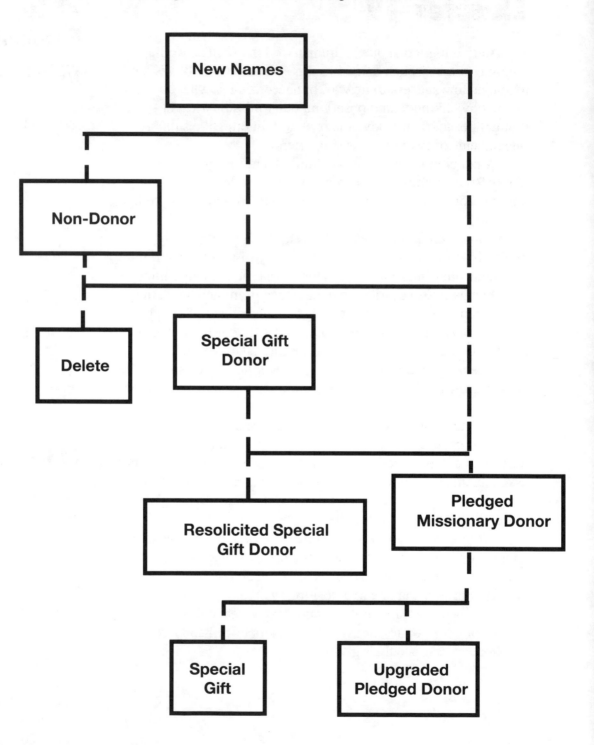

Three Categories of Giver

On the chart are three main categories: Non-Donor, Special Gift Donor, Pledged Donor. Let's look at each category separately.

The Non-Donor

In working with the non-donor, recognize that a no is never forever. Let's say he has been on your mailing list for a year. Last year when you asked him for support, he said no. Since circumstances change, you should approach him again. Hopefully, some, as shown on the chart, will become either Special Gift Donors or Pledged Donors. At some point, you may delete some who have declined to give several times.

Special Gift Donor

Special Gift Donors are a significant group of people who do not give monthly, quarterly, or annually with a pledge. Instead they help with special gifts. You have two goals with this group: the primary goal is to convert each to a Pledged Donor. The secondary goal is to secure second, third, and fourth special gifts. Resolicit this group for emergencies and other projects three or four times a year.

Examples of special needs are the birth of a baby, need for a new car, or training expenses.

Pledged Missionary Donors

Your pledged donors are your real base of support, but don't stop now. Regardless of whether they pledge monthly, quarterly, or annually, once a year they should be challenged to upgrade their giving. And that resolicitation should ideally be done eyeball to eyeball. This group should also be contacted to help in special emergencies, as they give above and beyond their pledged support. Steve Rentz of Campus Crusade even suggests securing a thirteenth gift from your monthly pledged donors.

In preparing to resolicit your donors, remember that you are seeking to bring each person to a point of maximum participation. Maximum participation level is achieved by doing two things: listening and asking to discover potential.

Review Each Pledged Giver

Name	Actual Pledged Support	Potential Pledged Support	Variance
Miss Suzette Casper	$15/month	$50/month	$35/month
Mr. Hugo Perez	$30/qtr.	$50/qtr.	$20/qtr.
Miss Julie Lockner	$50/year	$70/year	$20/year

If a person currently supports you at $40 per month, ask him to increase his pledge by $15 or $20 per month. If he currently gives $20 a month, ask for a $5 a month increase. If a person gives $100 a month, offer an open challenge, allowing him to increase at a level which he decides.

There is no right or wrong way to suggest an increase. Be careful that you do not aim too low, but use your judgment. It is much easier to get more money from an existing donor than to recruit a new donor. It is also more cost effective and time efficient.

Your primary strategy with each donor is to raise the frequency of his or her gift; the secondary goal is to raise the amount of his or her gift.

Review Your Special Gift Donors

Name	Actual Average Gift Support	Potential Pledged Support
Mr. Stephen Patterson	$25	$35 per month
Miss Edith Abayomi-Cole	$50	$70

Types of Donors

Remember that donors come in all shapes and sizes and temperaments. You make a big mistake if you treat them all the same. Instead, discover what type of donor each is.

Starters are people who like to start a project. They catch the vision quickly and want to be with you from the beginning.

Finishers are those who like the satisfaction of knowing that their gift pushed you over the top.

Project-oriented people are those who don't get much satisfaction from giving a gift to pay the utilities, rent, and so on. They are turned on by special projects.

Impulsive people are those who, when presented with an urgent challenge or need, respond quickly and gladly.

The programmed donor figures out his giving for the year on January 1. He locks his giving in, and your need, no matter how urgent or important, will fall on deaf ears. Ask that person for an appointment in mid-December, and ask for a commitment from him at that time for the next year.

It's important to keep notes on each giver and to know whether he or she likes to give regularly, to special projects, to emergencies, or has other giving patterns. Does he make a decision the first of the year? On a quarterly basis? When? Be there when he may be ready to give.

Self Guided Training

1. Go through your pledged donors, and identify all who have not increased the amount of their pledge in the last twelve months.

Prioritize that list by identifying each according to high-, medium-, and low-priority. Indicate what you think each could do in the way of increasing the amount of his pledge. Systematically visit or call each donor. Challenge him to upgrade his pledge. If a donor says he cannot increase his pledge, challenge him with specific projects and ask if he would give a special gift.

2. Check your list of special gift donors and prioritize that list by identifying each donor according to high-, medium-, and low-priority. Indicate what you want to challenge them to do in the way of a monthly pledged amount.

Systematically visit or call to ask each one if he or she will become a pledged donor. If he still cannot become a pledged donor, be sure to have specific projects you can offer him as a challenge and ask if he will give another special gift.

3. Check your list of non-donors and prioritize that list by identifying each as high-, medium-, or low-priority. In working with this group recognize that a no never means never.

Group
Guided

Training

Indicate what you think each non-donor could give in the way of a pledged amount. Systematically visit or call each and ask him if now he could become a monthly pledged donor. If he feels he cannot become a pledged donor, ask if he would give a special gift. Challenge him with a specific project.

Break into twos and role-play using the following scenarios. Switch partners, so everybody has a chance.

1. Rob Kearley is a successful Christian businessman and one of your pledged donors. He started supporting you eighteen months ago. Since then he has been promoted twice, and it appears that now would be a good time to resolicit him.

You have set the appointment with him by phone and have arrived for your appointment. After bringing each other up to date, you need to get down to business and ask him to increase his pledged support—take it from there in your role-play. Don't forget that if he says no, ask him for a special gift.

2. Tim Dearborn is a special gift donor. He has given financial gifts about three times a year during the last two years. Tim has just finished paying for his son's college education, and now might be a good time to see if he will become a pledged donor.

You have arrived for your appointment with him. You have brought each other up to date. Now you need to ask him to become one of your pledged donors—take it from there. Don't forget that if he says no, ask him for another special gift.

3. Lyn Matejczyk is an old college friend. When you first began raising support, you contacted her, but she could not help because she was unemployed at the time. Lyn is now employed, and it is a good time to transfer her from non-donor to pledged donor.

You have brought each other up-to-date. Now you need to get down to business to ask her to become one of your pledged monthly donors. If she says no, ask her for a special gift.

Conclusion

Chapter 21

"The ministry of deputation should be based upon and begin, as all other ministries, with prayer!" —Dr. Earnest Gambrell

Andy was grateful for the many friends who had taken on his financial support, but he reminded himself that he was involved in a spiritual battle. His study of Ephesians 6 last night reminded him that Satan was opposed to the spread of the gospel. A spiritual battle requires a spiritual weapon, and that weapon is prayer. Because Satan has many attack strategies, Andy needed a whole host of prayer partners, even prayer warriors.

"Mr. Dillon, my name is Dr. Monteverde. The medical data is telling me that you are about to have a second heart attack." I was forty-seven years of age, and as far as I knew, I had never had my first heart attack. Now my life was hung in the balance. A third heart attack would probably have snuffed out my life.

A staff member of Moody radio heard about my condition and broadcast the news. Thousands of Christians were made aware of my condition and began to pray. Phone calls poured in. Cards, flowers, and visitors arrived. Members of the hospital staff exclaimed, "We are not used to having a celebrity."

Who were those people? They were supporters and donors who through the years had prayed and given to our ministry. They were Christians who cared and believed that they could link me by prayer to the Great Physician. During those days in the hospital and while recuperating at home, I appreciated knowing that so many were supporting me in my need. God worked a miracle in my life and renewed my health.

When I think of prayer and the missionary raising support, I see two dimensions. The first dimension is the prayer life of the missionary. The second is the prayer support needed by the missionary to sustain his ministry.

First Dimension: The Prayer Life of the Missionary

Because this chapter appears near the end of the book, you may think I am saying, "When all else fails, pray." But there is nothing more contrary to the truth. Dr. Howard Hendricks has said, "Prayer is recognition that my need is not partial; it is total."

And 1 Thessalonians 5:17 is appropriate for support raising: "Pray without ceasing." *The New International Version* says, "Pray continuously." *The Living Bible* says, "Always keep on praying."

Because every effort should be bathed in prayer, let's review how to focus our praying.

Pray That the Lord Will Work
Above Our Strategies and Plans

Our churches have strategies for evangelism, for discipleship, and for church growth. And experience has convinced me that we also need strategies for support raising and prayer. But there is another overriding factor. Although God does work through our strategies, He is not tied to them. Paul reminds us in Ephesians 3:20 that He is capable of doing immeasurably more than all we ask or imagine, according to His power that is at work within us. A well-known saying is appropriate for us who raise support: "Work as if it all depends on you. Pray as if it all depends on God."

In the early days of our ministry we had no money, no staff, and no facilities—just a dream of bringing hope to the children of the inner city. Gradually, the Lord provided us with the needed resources. One was a meeting place.

We met on sidewalks, empty lots—any place we could find. Then we rented an old union hall that seemed ideal for our youth work. Unable to find anything more suitable, we prayed specifically for $10,000 to purchase that building by Christmas. By mid-December, no funds had come in, and we had little hope.

Our hopes were dashed further on December 21 when the building was set on fire and went up in flames. Where would we meet now? What would happen to the kids? What about our prayers for $10,000?

Meanwhile, we had promised to take the kids to winter camp. We loaded the children into buses behind that burned-out building. As the buses pulled away, I looked back at the charred union hall walls with a sick feeling. What would we do when we got back from camp? We had no place; we had no money. The ministry, in its infancy, seemed about to die.

But God in His sovereignty saw otherwise. While at camp we received word that an anonymous giver had sent a check for $10,000. Right to the penny and within the time frame of our prayers!

"Work as if it all depends on you. Pray as if it all depends on God."

In addition, God worked through that fire to lead us to negotiate the purchase of a building across the street from the burned-out union hall. We were amazed when the owners accepted our offer of $10,000 as a down payment. God had answered our prayers and given us a large, three-story building that was more than adequate for the expansion of our ministry. God works above our strategies. Keep planning but, above all, keep praying.

Remember that God "is able to do immeasurably more than all we ask or imagine, according to his power that is at work within us" (Eph. 3:20).

Pray for New Prospects

Pray that God will permit you to make contacts and gain favor with key people.

In the early days of our ministry I mentally listed key people with whom I hope to meet someday. They were people whom God had blessed who could help financially if they caught our vision. I prayed that someday they would help bring hope to inner city children and their families. In particular, I prayed for one man.

Several years later a friend urged me to attend a banquet of another non-profit organization. He mentioned that friends were hosting a table and were looking for another couple to attend.

Interested, I asked who the table host was. To my amazement, it was the man whom I had been praying to meet. I accepted the invitation and exchanged business cards with the table host. Several years later he toured our ministry facilities and eventually became a significant donor. God can perform miracles as you raise your support. Begin to pray today for key people to join your team.

Pray for the Right Words to Say

At times when I call to make appointments or ask for financial support, I am so nervous that I become tongue-tied. People may ask questions to which I am not sure how to respond, and it is at those times that I silently stop to pray.

I'm sure Nehemiah experienced similar feelings back in March or April, 444 B.C. As the king's cupbearer, he held a trusted position in the king's administration. In performing his duties, Nehemiah appeared daily before the king. One day, noting that Nehemiah appeared sad, the king asked him, "Why does your face look so sad when you are not ill? This can be nothing but sadness of heart."

Notice what Nehemiah did first. "I prayed to the God of heaven" (Neh. 2:4*b*). Then, "I answered the king" (v. 5).

It must have taken great courage for Nehemiah to share his vision for the rebuilding of Jerusalem. Like Nehemiah, there will be countless occasions when you will be plain scared. Pray and ask for God's wisdom.

Pray for Your Donors' Personal Needs

Bud Taylor of Source of Light Ministries, International, made this statement: "As you solicit the prayer support of others, you must accept the responsibility of praying for them."[1]

I hope you will not view people merely as prospects. That is cold and artificial. You are relating to people who have needs and who need someone to minister to them. You may be God's chosen person to meet those needs. Listen to them as they talk, and record their requests on your prayer list. Love them. Pray for them.

I had a delightful lunch recently with one of our donors. As we talked, he thanked me several times for the advice I had given him months before. "It was," he said, "exactly what I needed as I serve on our church board."

God has given each of us a tremendous ministry with donors. Pray for those who support you—for their careers, marriages, families, and churches.

The mission board of Pioneers offers the following suggestions for praying for one's donors.

1. Develop your own strategy and system for praying for each supporter.
2. Keep a picture album as you pray for families with children.
3. Make praying for donors a regular part of your devotions. To help you be systematic, put names of donors on different dates of the calendar, and pray for them on those dates.
4. In your prayer letters ask supporters to send you their specific prayer requests.

Pray for Miracles

Some years ago Torrey Johnson, founder of Youth For Christ, visited Inner City Impact for the first time. We spent the day together as he toured our facility and ministered to our staff. That afternoon we sat in my car outside the ICI headquarters, and he said, "Bill, tell me about the miracles. I want to hear about the miracles of this ministry."

I told him some miracles of the ICI ministry and was reminded that prayer activates a powerful God. It unleashes His resources to accomplish His purposes. Prayer shows how inadequate we are and brings a heart full of praise back to the Author and Finisher of our faith.

Psalm 44:3 states, "It is not by their sword that they won the land, nor did their arm bring them victory; it was your right hand, your arm, and the light of your face, for you loved them."

Pray for Boldness

Paul prayed for boldness as he proclaimed the gospel. In Ephesians 6:19, he says, "Pray also for me, that whenever I open my mouth, words may be given me so that I will fearlessly make known the mystery of the gospel." We need that boldness as we present our support needs.

Pray for Safe Travel

For some missionaries, travel means going thousands of miles by car and by air. So pray for safe passage and weather conditions, and that the car will work. We drive defensively and pray that the Lord will protect us from reckless drivers.

A former pastor tells the story of a friend who woke up in the middle of the night and felt compelled to pray specifically for his pastor. When the pastor returned, he learned of the man's middle-of-the night prayer at exactly the time he was in a situation of danger.

When a missionary has a support team of prayer warriors, the Holy Spirit will burden them to action at exactly the times when the prayers are needed, although the one praying may be unaware of the needs. That is a miracle—and the results that follow will be miracles as well.

Pray for God's Guidance and Blessing

Dr. Gambrell indicates that "Missionaries have driven many miles and gone to some churches where God did not want them. They wasted time and money. . . . The ministry of deputation is not a happenstance ministry. Just as surely as God calls a certain person to be missionary to a certain country, He also has certain churches that He selects to support that ministry. Therefore, it is important that the missionary seeks God's guidance for open doors and invitations to share his burden."[2]

Second Dimension:
The Prayer Support Needed by the Missionary

Missionaries need the consistent prayer support of family, friends, and the body of Christ. We are in a spiritual battle, and spiritual battles need spiritual weapons. Prayer is one of those weapons.

In many corners of the world today ordinary men are doing an extraordinary task for Jesus Christ. Part of the secret is that they are bathed in faithful prayer by God's dear saints in the homeland. Many people do not realize the extent of the battle Satan wages. "Our struggle is not against flesh and blood," writes the apostle Paul, "but against the rulers, against the authorities, against the powers of this world and against the spiritual forces of evil in the heavenly realms" (Eph. 6:12).

Because of the many demands on the missionary's time and the special need for prayer in his ministry, it may be your calling to uphold him by your prayers in a vital intercessory ministry. Take seriously the responsibility of carrying this prayer burden. When the missionary triumphs, his victory is yours to share.

The following suggestions from Greater Europe Mission may help your donors as they bring you before the Lord in prayer.[3]

Spend Time in Thanks for Your Missionaries
Thank God for their call and for their obedience to God's leading in their lives. Thank Him for the privilege of being involved with them in His work by upholding them in prayer.

Express thanks to God for the known blessings in their lives, for successes in the ministry in terms of conversions and spiritual growth. Thank God for His faithfulness in hearing your prayers on their behalf.

Pray for the Daily Lives of Your Missionaries
Their common problems are the same as yours, though you may not be made aware of them. Missionaries are subject to the same temptations and weaknesses you are.

Crossing an ocean does not solve the difficulties of daily living or make one a spiritual giant. Wherever you face problems, pray for your missionary in those areas of his life. Remember that missionaries are human.

Loneliness is only the beginning of the adjustment to living in a foreign culture. Pray that the missionary will be kept from pride, personality conflicts, and especially discouragement. Pray that he will be able to serve effectively with his fellow workers.

Pray That Barriers May Be Minimized

In an exceptional way the missionary needs patience in learning to do things the "foreign" way. He needs to gain rapport with people.

Pray that the efforts of Satan will meet with failure. In certain countries there is hostility or persecution. Pray that the Lord will keep His servants faithful in His Word and safe from the attacks of the enemy.

Pray That Your Missionaries Will Use Their Time Wisely

Missionaries are very busy people, and there are many demands on their lives. The task is always greater than their ability to serve, and it is very difficult to say no.

With many conditions beckoning for his attention, the missionary must make decisions as to what he will do and what he will leave undone. Pray that he will be discerning in the tasks he selects, and that his time will be spent in those activities that are most important in God's economy.

Pray, too, that your missionaries will be able to gain the needed rest for their bodies and minds, that they might be alert and effective in their work.

Pray That the Holy Spirit Will Lead Your Missionaries to Prepared Hearts

Although some hearts resist the gospel, many are hungry for spiritual reality. There are some in which the Holy Spirit has already been working. Pray that God will bring the missionary into contact with those people. Pray, too, that these hearts will be released from the grasp of doubt and fear and rebellion against God.

Pray for the Missionary's Children

Educating and disciplining children are frequently problems in a foreign culture. Some children have to live away from their families for their education. Different customs of child-rearing and discipline sometimes cause difficulties, and often the foreign culture magnifies ordinary everyday crises.

Pray for family peace and harmony, as the attitudes and behavior of the children may enhance or detract from the parents' ministry.

Pray Faithfully for Your Missionaries

Select a regular time to pray, and pray with diligence. When they really need your prayers, there is frequently no time to write an emergency prayer letter. What a blessing it is to a missionary to receive a letter saying, "We are praying for you daily." And make your prayers a time of carrying of their burdens to the Lord, not just a brief, "Lord, bless the missionaries."

Write to Them About Their Work

Keep track of their current prayer needs and find out which requests have been answered. If you have been praying about something daily for several months, write to ask how the Lord is working in that area. Ask about special needs. Some items cannot be shared with the public, and your missionary will appreciate your praying for those needs.

Pray for More Missionaries

Jesus told His disciples to pray that "the Lord of the Harvest would send forth laborers into the fields." There are never enough workers to complete the job. Young people are continuously preparing themselves for their lifetime occupations. Pray that God will call new resources into His service and that they will dedicate themselves in obedience to Him.

To help you get beyond the "God bless Bob and Janet" stage, Missionary Tech provides this helpful guide.[4] If you use it in your daily devotional time, it provides three requests per day. Take your pick, or use all three.

Sunday
Relationship with God
* Awareness of God's power
* Good times in His Word
* Conformity to His desire

Monday
Physical Needs
* General health
* Financial supply
* Strength and safety for work

Tuesday
Relationships with others
* Ability to submit to one another
* Honesty, openness
* Appreciation of others' gifts

Wednesday
Effective ministry
* Open doors for ministry
* Good use of time
* Personal witness

Thursday
Family life
* A healthy marriage
* Happy, secure children
* Good communication with parents, brothers, sisters

Friday
Emotional needs
* Healthy self-esteem
* Satisfaction in ministry
* Growth as a person

Saturday
Spiritual walk
* Assurance of Father's love
* Sense of Christ's presence
* Submission to Holy Spirit

Prayer/Advisory Group

Another prayer tool is the establishment of a Prayer/Advisory Group. Wycliffe offers these suggestions.[5]

Both the Old and the New Testaments give us models for praying before making plans and for making it a priority to have others pray with us. A Prayer/Advisory Group is a proven approach for using these scriptural principles. Some have found it to be the most significant thing they have done in support raising.

What Is a Prayer/Advisory Group?
A group of key partners commit themselves to pray for the ministry they share with you and to advise you on planning, setting goals and priorities, decision making, and so on. By participating as full partners they develop a sense of ownership

in ministry results. They also may act as advocates, make referrals, and fill special roles for which they are uniquely gifted or experienced.

Members live in close proximity to each other. When partners are scattered geographically, there may be more than one group. They may serve for a fixed time of partnership development and then disband or commit to long-term periods.

Purpose

The specific purpose is to get others to meet with you in worship, praise, and adoration before the Lord and then to pray, specifically, about problems, possible solutions, and priorities. The significance of this spiritual approach to mutual ministry cannot be overestimated.

Your confidence in being in the Lord's will, with His timing, and sharing the load with others, will significantly increase your effectiveness in meeting the needs of others, both among those who send you and among those to whom you are sent.

The Group's Leadership

Pray about a leader for the group. The success of this advisory group depends on the selection of the leader because he will be the key in making the group work effectively. The leadership of the Antioch church fasted and prayed before identifying Barnabas and Saul as their missionaries (Acts 11). Note there was a sense of responsibility to God, above the needs of the missionaries.

The Group's Function

The key is that the group feels a sending responsibility and ownership of the problems involved. So the leader needs to be approached from the perspective of responsibility to God for getting the Word to those who don't have it, rather than just to find solutions to the missionary's needs. Such an attitude significantly affects the group's level of commitment and its effectiveness.

The leader approaches others to be part of the group. The missionary will help, as needed, of course. But it should be clear from the beginning who the leader is and that the group's responsibility is ultimately to God.

Second, the missionary takes problems, concerns, and questions to the group, not his plans. He may have suggestions, ideas, and examples of things others have done to resolve similar problems. But the group should first be allowed to ask the Lord for His solution. Then the possibilities can be considered. Note: the plans taken to the group are not limited to finances or travel plans, but rather *everything* significantly affecting the partnership.

Third, it takes time for a group to begin functioning effectively. Much depends on the leader involved and where the other group members are in their level of education in missions, the depth of the relationship they already have with the missionary, and so on. It will take time to decide exactly what their role is, how they will meet their responsibilities, and how the missionary can best be accountable to them. It will take time for the leader to educate, motivate, and clarify roles. The missionary's availability to the leader is essential. So getting all those details set up and functioning will be high on your priority list.

Size of the Group

The level of commitment involved for all concerned is so high that a small group of five people may be best. But there is no established universal model. The same applies to who should be involved. If the group is primarily from one sending church, an individual from the church mission committee or an elder might be key members. If members of the group are from more than one church, involvement of key people from each church may be good. It will have the assurance that this is a special provision from God to keep you from feeling yours is a "Lone Ranger" ministry.

Partners in Ministry

If these people see their role as a special group with a specialized part in providing God's Word as part of the Great Commission, they will have a strong sense of ownership in mutual ministry.

The missionary's accountability will involve:

    a. Keeping the group fully aware of all situations concerning the partnership

    b. Carrying out plans as agreed

    c. Reporting progress, results, answers to prayer, and so on

233

In addition to the worship, prayer, and advice roles described above, the group's commitment to the missionary may involve advocacy roles such as:

a. Relating to others who may or may not be known to the missionary to obtain help in several areas of problem solving

b. Helping the missionary set appointments with key people, such as pastors, church leaders, mission committees, and so on

c. Taking active steps in the development of financial solutions, not necessarily from personal resources but by involving others

d. Assisting with scheduling, hosting, and follow-up of home meetings, or scheduling interviews with a variety of key people

Problems? It takes time and close cooperation. If you fear conflict of expectations between the Prayer/Advisory Group and the mission agency or churches not directly involved in the group, remember: *the group is advisory in nature, not directive.* If that is understood in the beginning, the group will be helpful to you when you face conflict of expectations and priorities from other sources.

There may be unusual situations where you believe that as the missionary, you should lead the group. Keep in mind that this is an advocacy relationship and if you do not have a third party as a leader, you won't feel entirely comfortable making certain suggestions. However, allow the Lord to lead you; having a group praying is the priority.

A Prayer/Advisory Group is a biblical concept. The Lord uses it significantly in the lives of senders and in missionaries' lives. Pray about it. If you think the Lord wants you to relate to one, think of the names of three potential leaders of the group. Pray about whom you should talk to first. Then decide how and when you might approach one of them about taking leadership of the advisory group.

Prayer/Advisory Group Plan of Action[6]

A. Suggested plan of action for the missionary

    1. Pray! Get others to pray with you.

    2. Choose names for prospective leader and group members from:

        a. Financial partners

        b. Prayer partners

        c. Potential financial partners

        d. Church leaders (pastor, elder, missions committee chairperson)

    3. Make the contact.

        a. By mail

            (1) You write

            (2) Someone else writes

        b. By phone

            (1) You call

            (2) Someone else calls (preceded by a letter)

    4. Obtain commitment.

    5. Equip and prepare the group leader.

    6. Set goals and a schedule for meeting goals (set target date).

    7. Follow up regularly (personal visits, phone calls, letters).

    8. Maintenance

        a. Newsletters (plan occasional reference to and recognize the group)

        b. Prayer letters (be sure to give feedback, answers to prayer, etc.)

        c. Consider using copies of your monthly financial statement to keep leader current. This allows him to carry responsibility of new effort in case of loss of partner, quota increase, etc.

        d. Send personal thank you notes regularly.

        e. Assure group is consulted before any decisions are made impacting the partnership.

As you raise support, claim Psalm 121. I call it The Missionary's Prayer as he raises support.

> *I lift up my eyes to the hills—*
> *where does my help come from?*
> *My help comes from the Lord,*
> *the Maker of heaven and earth.*
> *He will not let your foot slip—*
> *he who watches over you will not slumber;*
> *indeed, he who watches over Israel*
> *will neither slumber nor sleep.*
> *The Lord watches over you—*
> *the Lord is your shade at your right hand;*
> *the sun will not harm you by day,*
> *nor the moon by night.*
> *The Lord will keep you from all harm—*
> *he will watch over your life;*
> *the Lord will watch over your coming and going*
> *both now and forevermore.*

. . .dependence upon God in prayer is the ultimate way for doing spiritual work.

Daniel Bacon, U.S. Director of Overseas Missionary Fellowship (OMF), provides us with one last reminder:

> "Gratefully, technological developments have provided many helpful tools for missionary work, along with organizational structures that greatly facilitate the recruitment, sending, maintenance, and support of mission personnel. But. . . tools and organizations can never substitute for God's power which comes alone in answer to prayer. . . dependence upon God in prayer is the ultimate way for doing spiritual work."[7]

Before you is the exciting ministry of support raising. By now, you have not only developed positive feelings, but you are also beginning to acquire necessary skills. The final chapter will put it all into perspective as we discuss the question, "How do I begin?"

But before reading further, put down the book, slow down your pace, and shut off—as well as possible—all outside distractions. Take time to talk with your heavenly Father. Acknowledge your need of His guidance, and ask for His provision as you undertake this special ministry.

1. *Take your calendar and your list of prospects and donors and place a name under each date as a reminder to pray for them.*

2. *Start making a prayer album. Request pictures from your donors and place those pictures in a prayer album. Regularly pray for each donor as you review the album.*

3. *As you prepare your next prayer letter, invite those on your mailing list to send you specific prayer requests.*

4. *Develop your own daily prayer reminder program, or use the prayer guide in this chapter to send to your donors to remind them to pray for you.*

1. *Have each person complete the Self-guided Training questions, and bring a sample of what he has completed to class.*

2. *Have each person prepare his next prayer letter. In that letter he should to ask those on his mailing list to send specific prayer requests. Everyone should bring his letter. Break up into twos, and critique each other's letters.*

3. *Each person in the group develops his own daily prayer reminder program modeled after the one illustrated. In the group, have some show the prayer guides they developed.*

Notes

1. Bud Taylor, *Taking the P.U. out of Deputation* (Self-compiled pamphlet).
2. Ernest Gambrell, *The Ministry of Deputation* (Memphis: Fundamental Baptist Worldwide, 1987).
3. Greater European Mission, Wheaton, Illinois.
4. Missionary Tech Team, guide for prayer, 24 FRJ Drive, Longview, Texas 75602.
5 & 6. Discussions of Prayer/Advisory Group is adapted from Wycliffe Bible Translators.
7. Daniel W. Baker, From Faith To Faith, The Influence of Hudson Taylor on the Faith Missions Movement,
1983, pp. 185, 186.

Chapter 21

How Do I Begin?

After Andy had been on the field for some time, he set aside a day to pray. It was a time for him and the Lord to reflect and communicate. Opening his Bible, Andy turned to the Psalms and read promise after promise.

Many promises seemed to relate to his support-raising days, and reminded him of how glad he was that he had heeded the advice to build support by building relationships. He had watched a mighty God work far beyond his own strategy, creativity, and abilities. He bowed his head in thankfulness.

Andy remembered the dread he felt when he first realized he would have to raise support. He remembered his dilemma of whether or not to ask friends for support, followed by his commitment to meet people one-on-one.

That strategy had raised another series of fears—the fear of phoning to ask for appointments, the fear he felt on that first visit to Mr. Kern. He was downright scared when he started out, but the Lord gave him peace as he ventured by faith. Now that same faith was needed to accomplish his work on the field.

Andy continued reading and came to Psalm 18:6: "In my distress I called to the Lord; I cried to my God for help. From his temple he heard my voice; my cry came before him, into his ears." Andy had drawn strength from that scripture during his support raising. He knew he had direct access to an awesome God, and his prayers went directly to the ears of God.

Andy thought of all the people who were helping to meet his support needs—Rich and Tammy Doellstedt, Mary Wade, and others. Then he remembered that all his preparation and all his training in support raising had paid off. He had not struggled like other missionaries who gave up before raising their complete support. Andy was glad he had followed a plan.

Again, he bowed his head in prayer "Thank you, Lord, for giving me a plan and, above all, for working above that plan. Lord, You were with me every step of the way. I'm here on the field because You led and You've provided."

You have come a long way since you started in chapter 1. Now like Andy you have the option of choosing to follow a plan as you raise support. It is my prayer that the Lord will help you use the strategy in this book to raise your total support as efficiently as possible, in as short a time as possible.

239

Let's review the strategy for support raising from three perspectives: the new missionary, the veteran missionary, and the mission organization.

The New Missionary

As you launch your support ministry, review the first six chapters, which address cultivating a positive attitude toward support raising. Answer the questions at the conclusion of each chapter. Pray through areas of concern. Ask a trusted friend to counsel and pray with you as you proceed through the twelve steps of support raising.

Step 1: *Begin with Your Home Church*
Now that you understand the full scope of the support raising process, you are ready to call your pastor. Review the five goals (chapter 8) you want to achieve through a meeting with him. Then call and set an appointment. If you do not have a home church, proceed to step 2.

Step 2: *Determine to Whom You Will Go for Support*
Systematically list your acquaintances under each of the categories in chapter 9. Do not take shortcuts; carefully following this step will help you surface people whom God will use to meet your support needs.

Step 3: *Record and Catalog Prospects*
Record and catalog the names listed in step 2. Although it is time consuming and difficult (especially for those who are not detail-oriented), a thorough job now will save time and reap great benefits. Prioritize your list of prospects to select the top ten contacts. These are prospective donors on whom you will initially concentrate your support-raising efforts.

Step 4: *Mail Your First Prayer Letter*
Follow the guidelines in chapter 11 to write a prayer letter informing your friends about your missionary plans. Some people take hours to produce a simple letter, but you do not need to produce the perfect missive. Your time will be better spent preparing to meet people one-on-one.

Step 5: *Make Appointments*

Call the people on your top ten list to set appointments with prospective donors. Practice your presentation before phoning. (If you are having a hard time getting appointments see page 120 and review the trouble-shooting section.)

Step 6: *Conduct the Visit*

You've set an appointment for a certain day, time, and location. Before leaving for that first appointment, reread step 6 (chapter 13), and practice your presentation one more time. Pray that the Lord will guide you and be glorified during your time with the potential donor. (If you are failing to see people invest see page 147 and review the trouble-shooting section.)

Step 7: *Track Support*

After each appointment, add the name to your donor roster and systematically follow up on each contact according to the guidelines in chapter 14.

Step 8: *Say Thank You*

When you receive a support gift, write a thank you letter within twenty-four hours (or whatever time period is practical). Showing appreciation is key to maintaining your support, so don't neglect those who lovingly support you.

Step 9: *Conduct a Letter/Phone Strategy*

If you cannot visit a potential donor, you need to write a letter and follow up with a phone call. By reviewing this step, you will better understand how to proceed.

Step 10: *Expand Contacts*

There will come a time, as you pursue your support, when you will think you have run out of contacts. Don't be discouraged. Reread chapter 17, and take appropriate steps to build a base of future supporters. The people are out there. It is up to you to network through your friends and broaden your support base. Remember, expanding your number of contacts is possible.

Step 11: *Cultivate Your Support*

All of your support is in. You have reached your goal. You say, "Praise the Lord; support raising is done." Wrong! You should continue to cultivate your support and follow the principles laid out in chapter 18 to best accomplish that goal.

Step 12: *Resolicit for Support*

If you have done a good job of thanking your donors and building solid relationships, you will want to recontact some of them to ask if they are in a position to increase their giving. Also, some non-donors may be capable of helping at this time. This step ought to encourage you as you continue to build a strong support base for your long-term ministry.

Support raising is a challenge, and it is work, but the benefits are long range. Identifying friends, meeting with them, asking, cultivating, and resoliciting them will build a strong, long-range support base as you bring hope to a lost world.

The Veteran Missionary

You have already been in missionary service for a period of time and you have struggled with raising support. Chances are, your support needs are not met fully.

Maybe you are ready for home leave, and now is the time to adopt an efficient support-raising strategy. Maybe you are a home missionary, and you are ready to implement these steps to enhance your support. Perhaps you are on the field and separated from your support base. Whatever your circumstances, you need to do whatever is practical and workable.

 Self Guided Training

Reread the first six chapters to review how to cultivate a positive, expectant attitude toward support raising. Review the questions at the conclusion of each chapter and pray about areas of concern. Seek a trusted friend to counsel and pray with you as you progress through the twelve-step strategy of raising personal support.

Step 1: *Begin with Your Home Church*

Hopefully, you have already established a positive relationship with your home church, but a review of step 1 will help you strengthen that relationship. If you failed to begin in your home church when you started support raising, it is never too late.

Now that you understand the process of support raising, review the five goals you want to achieve when you meet with your pastor. Call him to set an appointment.

Perhaps a different pastor has come to the church since you met with the former pastor. Follow the guidelines in chapter 8 to share your vision with the new pastor and seek his endorsement of your ministry.

Step 2: *Determine to Whom You Will Go for Support*

How thoroughly did you develop a list of potential donors when you started raising support? How many new contacts have you made since those early days?

Go back and identify all the contacts the Lord has given you. Systematically list acquaintances in each category in step 2 to surface the names of people God will use to meet your support needs. Make a thorough list; do not take shortcuts here. If you are married, you and your spouse should combine your contacts.

Step 3: *Record and Catalog Prospects*

Reorganize your existing list of donors and prospects using the information in chapter 10. This may be time consuming, but a thorough job now will save you time and reap support benefits.

When the list of prospects and donors is organized, prioritize your top ten contacts from two sources: existing donors and potential donors (current non-donors).

Step 4: *Mail Your Prayer Letter*

As a veteran missionary, your have sent out many, many prayer letters. Continue to send monthly prayer letters to your supporters. Since such letters primarily are informational, be careful that you do not turn the monthly letter into an appeal letter.

Keep a diary throughout the month to collect ideas and stories to include in the letter when you are ready to write it. Evaluate past prayer letters according to the guidelines given in chapter 11. Invite friends to evaluate the letters from their objective viewpoints.

Step 5: *Make Appointments*

Practice your phone presentation according to the guidelines in chapter 12 in preparation for calling potential donors. Then systematically call the people on your top ten list to set appointments. (If you are having a hard time getting appointments see page 120 and review the trouble-shooting section.)

Step 6: *Conduct the Visit*

Now you have set the day, time, and location for an appointment. Before leaving for that first appointment, reread step 6 and practice your presentation one more time.

Because you will call some who are already donors and others who are currently non-donors, you need to clarify your strategy. Your goal for the donor is to express appreciation for his partnership with you in ministry and to encourage him to increase the amount of his support. Your goal for the non-donor is to share your excitement for the ministry and challenge him to start supporting you. Pray that the Lord will give you wisdom and be glorified in the meeting. (If you are having a hard time getting people to invest see page 147 and review the trouble-shooting section.)

Step 7: *Track Support*

After each appointment add the names to your donor roster and systematically follow up each contact.

Because some donors have supported you for a period of time, bring your donor roster up to date, and review ways to challenge and cultivate your existing donor base.

Step 8: *Say Thank You*

Within twenty-four hours, write a thank you letter for each gift received. Your appreciation is a key to maintaining support.

Step 9: *Conduct a Letter/Phone Strategy*

When you cannot visit a potential donor personally, write a letter and follow up with a phone call. Review the strategy of step 9 in chapter 16.

Step 10: *Expand Contacts*

Running out of potential donors probably is not a new experience for you. Don't get discouraged. All missionaries come to that point at some time in their missionary career.

A missionary on home leave needs to maximize his contacts and build the network of potential donors. Reread chapter 17, and take the appropriate steps to build a base of future supporters. The people are out there. It is up to you to network through your friends and broaden that base.

Step 11: *Cultivate Support*

The principles and ideas in chapter 18 teach you how to cultivate your support. Even while you are on the field, there are things you should do regularly.

Step 12: *Resolicit for Support*

I am certain that there are donors on your list who are waiting to be asked again. They have given, and you have maintained contact. They believe in what you are doing, but now they need to be resolicited.

Your home leave will be an ideal time to reestablish contact and challenge them to upgrade their giving. And don't forget those non-donors who might now be in a position to help.

The Mission Organization

Your mission can use this book as a tool to train both new and veteran missionaries. I suggest you proceed with four steps:

Step 1: Identify one person in your mission organization to be the trainer. Whether you already have a person serving in that capacity or need to select a person, he should:

- Be committed to prepare people for a support ministry of one-on-one visits.
- Have the ability to teach others.
- Have the ability and desire to hold others accountable.

Step 2: I assume the trainer has been a missionary and is acquainted with support raising. However, he needs to experience everything he will teach so that it becomes second nature to him. Therefore, he should study the support strategy outlined in this book and follow the suggestions above under The Veteran Missionary.

Step 3: When the trainer understands the support-raising strategy and has experienced it firsthand, he will organize a group of missionaries to study this book and train them using the Group-Guided Training program at the end of each chapter.

Group
Guided

Training

Step 4: The trainer will follow up with those who graduate from the course and hold each accountable on a weekly basis until 100 percent of his support has been pledged.

There are two forms that are absolutely necessary for monitoring the missionary's support. See step 7 (chapter 14) for instructions on how to use the Support-Raising Report and Donor Roster.

As a mission you will train not only your new missionaries but also the veteran missionaries. This training can take place prior to home leave or in conjunction with it.

Your goal is to equip your people to raise support in as efficient a manner and as short a time as possible. The funds are out there. It is our job to pray, to strategize, and work diligently to assist our missionary staff in becoming fully supported.

You can do it. And He can do it. Your hard and diligent work, along with the Lord's special provision, makes support raising possible. (As you monitor your missionaries and find those who are struggling to get appointments, read Chapter 12, page 120 and review the trouble-shooting section. For those failing to see people invest after meeting with them, see Chapter 13 page 147 and review the trouble-shooting section.)

Support raising is a ministry that starts and ends with relationships

A Word to the Potential Missionary

If you have thought about missionary service but raising support scares you, I pray that this book will help you view the process positively. As you raise support, God will increase your faith in miraculous ways. He will lead you to new friends and through new experiences. When an effective strategy is followed, support raising, rather than being a nightmare, becomes an exciting journey of spiritual growth. And if that is God's will for you, it is a process you won't want to miss.

A Word to Pastors, Mission Committees, Mission Teachers, and Others

God will bring across your path His choice servants who are looking for guidance as they follow the path to the mission field. This book offers the guidance, but the prospective or veteran missionary may need your encouragement as he works through the steps. You may become his teacher or discipler. He may need to pray and talk about his experiences with you. He may need to become accountable to you. I encourage you to be sensitive to the needs of that individual and stand in the gap with him.

In Conclusion

This book emphasizes building relationships as a number-one priority. I hope you caught that! There are no shortcuts, and there is no quick fix. If there were, I would have passed that secret formula on to you at the beginning.

Support raising is a ministry that starts and ends with relationships—the missionary cares about and ministers to supporters, and they in turn minister to the missionary.

Be assured that you are a valuable part of the Lord's work and that you are needed on the mission field. So don't be sidetracked. Follow the twelve-step support-raising strategy with a joyful, confident heart. Do all in your power to complete your support and get to the field as soon as possible.

As you raise support, fear may paralyze you at times. It can take many forms, including the fear of setting appointments, the fear of calling back a person who made a pledge and has yet to send the first gift, or the fear of asking for referrals. When gripped by fear, people have a tendency to procrastinate. Be careful that doesn't happen to you.

You may tend to fall back on an impersonal tool such as letter writing, instead of building one-on-one relationships. I assure you that that approach will set you back several months, if not years. You need to meet personally with as many potential donors as possible.

With a willing heart and the twelve-step strategy, pray for God to work above your efforts. He is faithful. Because He has called you, He will provide. But He is dependent on you to do your part.

We need to see God's fingerprints all over our support plan. As you proceed say:

> *Come and see what God has done, how awesome his works in man's behalf! (Ps. 66:5)*

> *The Lord has done this, and it is marvelous in our eyes. (Ps. 118:23)*

God bless you as you are involved in the exciting ministry of people raising.

Bibliography

Some of the following comes from the book
Support Raising Handbook — A Guide for Christian Workers; Brian Rust/Barry McLeish; 1984

Suggested Reading

The following books, periodicals and papers are highly recommended for further reading. They are listed by categories pertinent to missionary support raising.

History

Grubb, Norman. C. T. Studd. Grand Rapids, Mich.: Zondervan, 1941. Kane, J. Herbert. *Life and Work on the Mission Field.* Grand Rapids, Mich.: Baker, 1980.

Latourette, Kenneth. *A History of Christianity.* Vols. 1. New York: Harper & Row, 1975.

——-. *A History of the Expansion of Christianity.* Vols 1-2, 7. Grand Rapids: Zondervan, 1971.

Powell, Luther. *Money and the Church.* New York: Association Press, 1962. Steer, Roger. *George Muller: Delighted in God!* Carol Stream, Ill.: Harold Shaw, 1981

Taylor, Mr. & Mrs. Howard. *The Story of the China Inland Mission.* Vol. 1. London: Marshall Morgan and Scott, 1983.

Taylor, Mrs. Howard. *William Borden.* Chicago: Moody, 1980.

Stewardship

Ellul, Jacques. *Money & Power.* Translated by LaVonne Neff. Downers Grove, Ill.: InterVarsity Press, 1984.

McClanen, Don. *Stewardship Challenges for Ministering to Affluent Persons.* Ministry of Money, Inc. (MOMI), 11301 Neelsville Church Rd., Germantown, MD 20874.

O'Connor, Elizabeth. *Letters to Scattered Pilgrims.* New York: Harper & Row, 1979; especially chapter two, "On Money" and chapter three, "More on Money."

Snow, Catherine. Writing a Money Autobiography. MOMI, 11301 Neelsville Church Rd., Germantown, MD 20874.

Vinkemulder, Yvonne. *Enrich Your Life.* Downers Grove, Ill.: InterVarsity Press, 1972.

Webley, Simon. *How to Give Away Your Money.* Downers Grove, Ill.: InterVarsity Press, 1978.

Weborg, John. *God & Mammon.* MOMI, 11801 Neelsville Church Rd., Germantown, MD 20874.

Support Audiences/Case Statement

Engel, James. *How Can I Get Them to Listen?* Grand Rapids: Zondervan, 1977.

Ries, Al, and Trout, Jack. *Positioning: The Battle for Your Mind.* New York: McGraw-Hill, 1980.

Writing Letter/Communication Tools

Mack, Karin, and Skjei, Eric. *Overcoming Writing Blocks.* Los Angeles: J.P. Tarcher, 1979.

Pocket Pal. International Paper Co., P.O. Box 100, Church Street Station, New York, NY 10046.

Strunk, William, Jr., and White, E. B. *The Elements of Style.* New York: Macmillan, 1979.

Winkler, G.P., ed. *The Associated Press Stylebook.* Write to AP Newsfeatures, 50 Rockefeller Plaza, New York, NY 10020.

Zinsser, William. *On Writing Well.* 2d ed. New York: Harper & Row, 1980.

General

Hales, Edward, and Youngren, Alan. *Your Money, Their Ministry: A Guide to Responsible Christian Giving.* Grand Rapids: Eerdmans, 1981.

Kurzid, Carol. *Foundation Fundamentals: A Guide for Grantseekers.* New York: Foundation Center, 1981.

Perri and Ardman. *Woman's Day Book of Fund Raising.* New York: St. Martin's Press, 1980.

Peters, Thomas J., and Waterman, Robert H., Jr. *In Search of Excellence.* "Close to the Customer," chapter 6. New York: Harper & Row, 1982.

Piguet, Leo. *Fund Raising.* National Institute for Campus Ministries, 1979.

Sharpe, Robert F. *Before You Give Another Dime....* Nashville: Nelson, 1979.

Periodicals

Communicator's Journal—A bimonthly magazine of applied communications. Frequently contains articles helpful to anyone in the communications field. P.O. Box 602, Downtown Station, Omaha, NE 68101.

Currents—The monthly publication for members of the Council for Advancement and Support of Education (CASE). CASE is an association designed to help public information and fundraising professionals in chiefly nonprofit educational institutions. Articles appearing in *Currents* cover topics related to fundraising and public information/relations in this field. Council for Advancement and Support of Education, Suite 400, Eleven Dupont Circle, Washington, D.C. 20036

Nonprofit World Report—The bimonthly magazine of the Society for Nonprofit Organizations. Contains articles and tips on everything from fundraising to communications. The Society for Nonprofit Organizations, 9 Odana Ct., Madison, WI 53719.

Organizations

Evangelical Development Ministry, 3870 Antigua Drive, Dallas, TX 75244, (214) 484-6432.

Evangelical Council for Financial Accountability (ECFA), P.O. Box 17456 Washington, D.C. 20041.

Christian Management Association, P.O. Box 4638, Diamond Bar, CA 91765.

The Ministry Leadership Group, 7412 Club View Drive, Highland, CA 92346, (909)864-2798, fax(909)864-2494.

Manual for Today's Missionary — Marjorie A. Collins; 1986;
William Carey Library, P.O. Box 40129, 1705 N. Sierra Bonita
Avenue, Pasadena, CA 91104.

Who Cares About the Missionary — Marjorie A. Collins;
1975; Don Wardell, Box 325, Winona Lake, IN 46590.

Tapes

"Personal Finances--A Biblical Basis," by Earl Pitts--four 90-minute
cassette tapes with printed work sheets offering challenging teaching
on finances. Send $14.50 (subject to change), postage included (or
$16.50 Canadian) to: Earl Pitts, P.O. Box 1324, Cambridge, Ontario,
N1R7G6 Canada.

"Raising Personal Support, A Biblical Approach to Fund Raising," by
Scott Morton, The Navigators, P.O. Box 6000, Colorado Springs, CO
80934 U.S.A. An excellent video tape series which has benefited many
mission agencies and missionaries.

Books

Debt-Free Living: How to Get Out of Debt & Stay Out, by Larry
Burkett; Moody Press, Chicago, Illinois U.S.A. 1989.

Friend Raising — Building A Missionary Support Team That Lasts,
Betty Barnett; YWAM Publishing, a division of Youth With A
Mission, P.O. Box 55787, Seattle, Washington 98155 U.S.A.

*The Friendship Factor: How to Get Closer to the People You Care
For,* by Alan Loy McGinnis; Augsburg Publishing House,
Minneapolis, Minnesota U.S.A. 1979.

The Gift of Giving, by Wayne Watts; NavPress, P.O. Box 6000,
Colorado Springs, Colorado 80934 U.S.A. (excellent book on
generosity).

*God's Managers: A Budget Guide and Daily Financial Record Book
for Christians*, by Ray and Lillian Blair; Herald Press, Scottsdale,
Pennsylvania 15683 U.S.A. 1985.

Money, Sex & Power, The Challenge of the Disciplined Life, by
Richard J. Foster, Harper & Row Publishers, U.S.A. 1985 (deals with
money, its dark and light side).

Spiritual Warfare For Every Christian: How To Live in Victory and Retake the Land, by Dean Sherman; YWAM Publishing, a division of Youth With A Mission, P.O. Box 55787, Seattle, Washington 98155 U.S.A. 1990.

Stewardship Training Manual and Presentation Book, a helpful tool designed especially for YWAM missionaries to help them raise support and manage their finances by Godly principles, by Missions Network Center, Box 7, Elm Springs, Arkansas 72728-0007 U.S.A.

The Support-Raising Handbook: A Guide for Christian Workers, by Brian Rust and Barry McLeish; InterVarsity Press, Downers Grove, Illinois 60515 U.S.A. 1984 (includes many practical helps.)

Support Wise: How to Establish, Nuture, and Maintain a Long-term Financial Support Base, by Chris Stanton; Mission Bridge Books, 11300 Kamloops, Lakeview Terrace, California 991342, (818) 899-4289 (a practical "how to" workbook on making a support-raising presentation).

Wealth & Wisdom: A Biblical Perspective on Possessions, by Jake Barnett; NavPress, P.O. Box 6000, Colorado Springs, Colorado 80934 U.S.A. 1987 (excellent study of finances, emphasizing generosity).

Your Money/Their Ministry: A Guide to Responsible Christian Giving, by Edward J. Hales and J. Alan Youngren; Wm. B. Eerdmans Publishing Co., Grand Rapids, Michigan U.S.A. 1981 (includes sections on Christian fund raising, abuses and uses).

Serving As Senders, by Neal Pirolo; by Emmaus Road, International, Operation Mobilization Literature Ministry, 129 Southside Drive, P.O. Box 28, Waynesboro, GA 30830, 1991.

Moody Press, a ministry of the Moody Bible Institute,
is designed for education, evangelization, and edification.
If we may assist you in knowing more about Christ and
the Christian life, please write us without obligation:
Moody Press, c/o MLM, Chicago, Illinois 60610.

WILLIAM P. DILLON

A PRACTICAL GUIDE TO RAISING SUPPORT

PEOPLE RAISING

PEOPLE RAISING KIT CONTENTS:

- Four 90 Minute Video Tapes
- Four 90 Minute Audio Cassettes
- Study Guide
- Copy of *People Raising: A Practical Guide To Raising Support*

FURTHER INFORMATION:

William P. Dillon, President
Resource Management
Consultants

(Toll Free) 1-877-611-PEOPLE
Visa and Mastercard Accepted
Wmdillon@hotmail.com

VISIT US ON THE WEB:

www.peopleraising.com

New! Now Available People Raising Seminar on Video

Great news! All of the valuable information in *People Raising: A Practical Guide To Raising* is now available in an expanded kit.

William P. Dillon, author of this increasingly popular book, now presents the *People Raising Seminar* in video and audio format.

This well-organized seminar is fast-paced, motivating, and stimulating. Dillon incorporates power point visuals, role playing, questions from the audience, and well-designed small group discussions.

The goal of the seminar is to help the viewer reduce not only the fears of raising support but also dramatically reduce the time necessary to raise the needed funds. Even experienced fundraisers can gain insights on how to expand their lists and upgrade needed support. Helpful practical suggestions make it easier and more comfortable to bring contacts to a point of decision.

Whether you're a new missionary, or the Director of Development, the *People Raising Kit* is the perfect tool to reduce your fears and time you spend raising support.

"This is beautiful. It's Biblical, practical, and now we have the opportunity of getting into the author's mind and heart and seeing how to raise people who care about what God is doing around the world."

Dr. Ron Blue, CAM International

Another Great Title by Moody Press

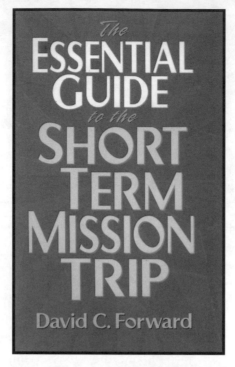

The Essential Guide to the
Short Term Mission Trip

A richly detailed, step by step approach to planning a successful short-term mission experience. This book has done an excellent job of practically explaining what it takes for your short-term mission trip to be a Kingdom-building experience.

This book is for short-term missionaries and their team leaders. Team leaders, whether ordained or from the laity, will benefit from it's advice on how to build, plan, and lead a group of people with differing interests and objectives, molding them into one team with the singular purpose of building the kingdom of God as servant disciples. But it is also for the participant in that team. It will help the short term mission worker to focus on why he or she is going and offer practical tips on how to make the trip more fulfilling.

"This book fills the needed gap in helping to prepare and train teams. It helps keep them productive for the kingdom while focusing on their mission."   --Greg Parsons, Executive Director,
US Center for World Mission.

ISBN: 0-8024-2526-7, Paperback